T0213022

Whitestein Series in Software Agent Technologies and Autonomic Computing

Series Editors:
Marius Walliser
Stefan Brantschen
Monique Calisti
Stefan Schinkinger

This series reports new developments in agent-based software technologies and agent-oriented software engineering methodologies, with particular emphasis on applications in the area of autonomic computing & communications.

The spectrum of the series includes research monographs, high quality notes resulting from research and industrial projects, outstanding Ph.D. theses, and the proceedings of carefully selected conferences. The series is targeted at promoting advanced research and facilitating know-how transfer to industrial use.

About Whitestein Technologies

Whitestein Technologies is a leading innovator in the area of software agent technologies and autonomic computing & communications. Whitestein Technologies' offering includes advanced products, solutions, and services for various applications and industries, as well as a comprehensive middleware for the development and operation of autonomous, self-managing, and self-organizing systems and networks.
Whitestein Technologies' customers and partners include innovative global enterprises, service providers, and system integrators, as well as universities, technology labs, and other research institutions.

www.whitestein.com

Defence Industry Applications of Autonomous Agents and Multi-Agent Systems

Michal Pěchouček
Simon G. Thompson
Holger Voos
Editors

Birkhäuser
Basel · Boston · Berlin

Editors:

Michal Pěchouček
Department of Cybernetics
Faculty of Electrical Engineering
Czech Technical University
Technicka 2
CZ 166 27 Prague 6
Czech Republic
pechouc@labe.felk.cvut.cz

Simon G. Thompson
Research and Venturing
BT. Labs, PP12, MLB1
Adastral Park
Suffolk IP45AF
United Kingdom
simon.2.thompson@bt.com

Holger Voos
Faculty for Electrical Engineering and Computer Science
University of Applied Sciences Ravensburg-Weingarten
P.O. Box 1261
D-88214 Weingarten
Germany
voos@hs-weingarten.de

2000 Mathematical Subject Classification: 68T05, 68T35, 68T45

Library of Congress Control Number: 2007938077

Bibliographic information published by Die Deutsche Bibliothek
Die Deutsche Bibliothek lists this publication in the Deutsche Nationalbibliografie;
detailed bibliographic data is available in the Internet at <http://dnb.ddb.de>.

ISBN 978-3-7643-8570-5 Birkhäuser Verlag AG, Basel – Boston – Berlin

© 2008 Birkhäuser Verlag, P.O. Box 133, CH-4010 Basel, Switzerland
Part of Springer Science+Business Media
Printed on acid-free paper produced from chlorine-free pulp. TCF ∞
Printed in Germany

ISBN 978-3-7643-8570-5   e-ISBN 978-3-7643-8571-2

9 8 7 6 5 4 3 2 1   www.birkhauser.ch

Contents

Preface

The future capabilities of modern armed forces are often characterized by terms like "Network Centric Warefare" (NCW), "Network-Enabled Capabilities" (NEC) or "Network-Based Defence" (NBD). All of these approaches share the common idea that the application of modern communication and information processing technologies will result in a very efficient and effective utilization of resources available to commanders. By utilizing state of the art techniques from Electronics and Computer Science defence theorists hope to be able to create force structures that are more responsive, cost effective and agile than their opponents; if knowledge is power NCW seeks to translate battle field information into fighting power.

The first step toward realizing these visions is to be able to gather, distribute, correlate, process and inference over the information generated by field assets such as sensors and personnel as well as information held in databases, practice manuals and logistics information systems. Herein, the most important resource is information and hence information gathering, distribution and processing is the key factor for mission effectiveness. The resulting scenarios of networked armed forces require

- a flexible and very reliable interaction infrastructure which collect and process information to assist decision making
- the integration of unmanned systems in the battlefield
- the organization of agile logistics
- the modeling and prediction of adversary intent
- intelligent training

Most of these applications run in highly decentralized and heterogeneous environments and/or require embodiment of autonomous, intelligent decision making. These characteristics make the defense application domain appropriate for the deployment of the technologies, techniques and algorithms provided by researchers working in the fields of Intelligent Agents, Autonomous Agents and Multi-Agent Systems (jointly referred to as AAMAS technologies).

These days AAMAS researchers provide high quality of fundamental research results in various sub-fields of agent technology such as formal models of cooperation and coordination, game theory and mechanism design, models of argumentation and negotiation and formal (logical) reasoning about multi-actor scenarios. As well as working on these theoretical topics the AAMAS community also addresses application oriented subfields such as distributed planning, collective robotics, information retrieval and distributed learning, modeling trust and reputation among actors, intentional modeling, task and resource allocation or multi-agent modeling or simulation. Readers are referred to e.g., international conference on Autonomous Agents and Multi-agent Systems (http://www.aamas-conference.org/)

[1,2] and IEEE/WIC/ACM International Conference on Intelligent Agents Technology (http://www.cs.sjsu.edu/wi07/iat/) [3], Cooperative Information Agents workshop series (http://www-ags.dfki.uni-sb.de/~klusch/IWS-CIA-home.html) [4] or International Conference on Industrial Applications of Holonic and Multi-Agent Systems (http://gerstner.felk.cvut.cz/HoloMAS/2007/) [5].

AAMAS technologies are not investigated in isolation. AAMAS research is supported not only by universities, research institutes and national/international grant agencies but also by important industrial stakeholders, the defense industry in particular. Military organizations are traditionally a supporter and an early adopter of innovative technologies and AAMAS technologies are no exception. While involvement of conventional industries in AAMAS research emphasizes on fast return on investment, defense support and interest in AAMAS technologies facilitates slightly longer adoption lifecycle. This approach gives a balance between time and resources for fundamental research, prototyping and demonstration as well as experimental deployment of a particular research idea or concept. At the same time as providing an appropriate domain of application of AAMAS techniques defence applications provide AAMAS researchers with stimulating new challenges in the shape of the constraints of bandwidth, energy and processing power available to their applications.

As the knowledge of successful applications of agent technology in military domains is dispersed in specialized workshops and symposia, we have brought these reports together here to provide a clear picture of the state of the art in this field at this time, and to promote further investigation and interest in this increasingly important topic.

This book is a selected collection of recent published and refereed papers drawn from workshops and other colloquia held in various venues around the world in the last two years. The book logically follows the effort of the editors towards communicating the research results to the industrial community and trying to bridge the gap between researchers and industrial engineers. When editing the book, the editors leverage their experiences in establishing the AAMAS Industry track back in 2005 [6], organizing the DAAMAS workshop informally in New York in 2004 and formally in Utrecht in 2005 [7] and working in the Defence Technology Centre programs in the UK.

Papers in this book describe work in the development of command and control systems, military communications systems, information systems, surveillance systems, autonomous vehicles, simulators and HCI. The broad nature of the application domain is matched by the diversity of techniques used in the papers that are included in the collection. The collection provides, for the first time, an overview of the most significant work being performed by the leading workers in this area. It provides a single reference point for the state of the art in the field at the moment and will be of interest to Computer Science professionals working in the defense sector, and academics and students investigating the technology of Intelligent Agents that are curious to see how the technology is applied in practice.

As mentioned earlier the book is a collection of independent, unlinked chapters. The readers are welcome to read the chapters in the order of their choosing. In order to give some guidance, the book is organized in three loosely structured sections. The first four chapters describe multi-agent approaches to organization of the information infrastructure, data collection and resource matchmaking. This section is complemented with the application chapter on agent deployment in military logistics. The following three chapters provide technical information about agent deployment in the manned and unmanned air traffic control. The last three chapters of the collection are about the use of agents for simulation and training. The second and third sections are naturally overlapped by the chapter on simulation of fighter pilots.

The editors hope that the book will provide a valuable reference, will contribute to the discussion about exploitation potentials of agent technology in the defense industry and initiate implementation of further innovative applications and deployment exercises.

Michal Pěchouček, Simon Thompson and Holger Voos
Praha - Ipswich - Weingarten
October 2007

References

[1] P. Stone, G. Weiss (Eds.), *Proceedings of the fifth international joint conference on Autonomous agents and Multi-agent systems 2006.* ISBN:1-59593-303-4.

[2] F. Dignum, V. Dignum, S. Koenig, S. Kraus, M. Pechoucek, M. Singh, D. Steiner, S. Thompson, and M. Wooldridge (Eds.), *Proceedings of the Fourth international joint conference on Autonomous agents and Multi-Agent systems 2005.* 1407, ACM, ISBN:1-59593-093-0.

[3] T. Nishida, M. Klusch, K. Sycara, M. Yokoo, J. Liu, B. Wah, W. Cheung, and Y. M. Cheung (Eds.), *Proceedings of the 2006 IEEE/WIC/ACM International Conference on Intelligent Agent Technology.* Hong Kong, China, 18-22 December 2006. IEEE Computer Society 2006.

[4] M. Klusch, M. Rovatsos, T. R. Payne (Eds.), *Cooperative Information Agents X, 10th International Workshop, CIA 2006.* Edinburgh, UK, September 11-13, 2006, Proceedings, Lecture Notes in Computer Science 4149 Springer 2006, ISBN 3-540-38569-X.

[5] V. Mařík, D. C. McFarlane, P. Valckenaers (Eds.), *Holonic and Multi-Agent Systems for Manufacturing, First International Conference on Industrial Applications of Holonic and Multi-Agent Systems, HoloMAS 2003.* Prague, Czech Republic, September 1-3, 2003, Proceedings, Lecture Notes in Computer Science 2744 Springer 2003, ISBN 3-540-40751-0.

Whitestein Series in Software Agent Technologies, 1–13
© 2007 Birkhäuser Verlag Basel/Switzerland

Nexus: Self-organising Agent-based Peer-to-Peer Middleware for Battlespace Support

Alex Healing, Robert Ghanea-Hercock, Hakan Duman and
Michal Jakob

Abstract. The problem facing the security and defence communities is the
volume, complexity and timeliness of information. In particular the ability to
locate and access the right ICT service at the right time is crucial to achieving real-time responsiveness and situational awareness. The Nexus system is
a Peer-to-Peer (P2P) agent-based middleware that creates a fully distributed
and highly resilient Service Oriented Architecture (SOA). The combination
of a structured P2P overlay network and autonomous service discovery, de-
livers a powerful capability to support real-time operations in either security
or defence applications. This paper outlines the overall architecture of the
Nexus system and its application in a defence scenario with a detailed review
of the service selection algorithm utilised, termed Mercury. Mercury provides
an autonomous, efficient and distributed service selection framework and collaborative algorithms for SOA construction and real-time adaptation.

1. Introduction

Future military force requirements will demand a migration towards ever increasing
levels of ICT automation and self-organising capability. This is a simple function
of reduced administrative support, increasingly complex networked systems and
the ever shrinking time available for response. In addition the need for shared situational awareness across tactical and coalition spheres makes manual service configuration a logistic nightmare. This chapter reviews a solution based on combing
the best features of P2P and SOA approaches to create a self-* service platform.
An overview of the Nexus autonomic middleware is first given, followed by an
in-depth technical discussion of one of its components - adaptive service selection.

2. Approach

The first phase of the Nexus project [7, 9] demonstrated the value of an agent-based P2P middleware for the discovery and fusion of NEC services. The Nexus middleware is based on three key paradigms: P2P computing, autonomous agents and SOA [5]; all of which have been identified as key components of future NEC network architectures [1]. Existing implementations of SOA, as applied in the civil domain, suffer from several issues that make them unsuitable for volatile environments. These include centralized service discovery and process orchestration, and fixed manually specified workflows. These factors lead to fragile, non-adaptive and difficult-to-maintain network applications. The aim is to develop a hardened, agent-based SOA implementation that meets the strict reliability requirements of the NEC domain and accommodates the needs of network-centric information fusion applications. More specifically, the following capabilities are being developed either as a direct part of Nexus II middleware or by integrating technologies from other projects within the Hyperion cluster [2]:

- Seamless and reliable service delivery in volatile environments
- Request prioritisation and load-balancing
- Resilience to volatility of the underlying network infrastructure: by adopting a peer-to-peer architecture Nexus maintains its operability even if a large subset of services or the network itself becomes unavailable.
- Decentralised service discovery whereby networked resources are discovered based on their advertised properties and real-time information regarding their dynamic attributes without reliance on a centralised repository.
- Semantic and adaptive service selection based on dynamically maintained quality-of-service profiles.
- Proactive monitoring and automated service substitution: The state of services is actively monitored and should a failure occur the failed resource is rapidly substituted with the closest alternative, preserving the overall capability.
- Filtering of information services based on their semantic relevance to the user as well as imposing some structure at the messaging layer of the middleware allowing bandwidth to be conserved.

In order to offer the necessary resilience Nexus adopts an entirely decentralised approach. At the lowest level, a P2P overlay network is constructed, either directly or indirectly, connecting each of the nodes in the network running Nexus with each other. Similar to [12, 18], the overlay network is then coupled with component-model technologies which in our case offer a Publish/Subscribe (Pub/Sub) structured messaging layer from which higher level management of the network can be constructed.

Each Nexus node can host a number of services and these are made available through the middleware by means of advertising their associated metadata on the messaging layer. Users of Nexus are required to connect to only a single node from where the middleware allows them to discover resources throughout the network and manage their view and usage of the information services according to their requirements.

We adopt the Autonomic Computing [10, 13] paradigm which introduces self-* capabilities to allow Nexus to intelligently and autonomously handle the dynamic environment for which it is intended; including changing requirements of users, unreliable service availability, or failure of the underlying physical network.

Nexus is entirely implemented in the Java programming language and relies on several open-source third party libraries. In particular, the current embodiment of Nexus builds on an open-source P2P implementation of Java Message Service (JMS) [8] to provide the majority of the functionality of the bottom two layers in Fig. 1.

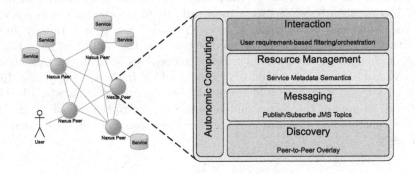

FIGURE 1. Nexus Autonomic Middleware Architecture.

IP multicast is used to discover other Nexus peers and construct the overlay whereby each peer advertises itself on a common channel thus allowing each peer to know the presence of others. JMS topics provide Pub/Sub functionality for the message-oriented component of Nexus and allow for information service advertisements to be structured in their transmission across the network. Each peer acts as a message broker and routes messages to peers that are subscribed to the topic on which the message was published. The topics can be structured into a hierarchy, allowing one to subscribe to only messages concerning a specific subset of services. To some degree, the semantics relating to the service descriptions in the resource layer can be exposed to the messaging structure in the layer below. The routing of messages throughout the overlay can therefore be linked to the semantic relevance of the resources that the messages describe to each peer. This capability is of value in reducing the overall bandwidth requirements of the supported applications and services.

There are numerous aspects of the architecture to which autonomic computing principles may be applied. For example, the driving of the aforementioned messaging structure by the service metadata may be an autonomous process. At the lowest level, the overlay network is self-organising in that changes to the topology are dealt with seamlessly allowing for new peers joining the network to be discovered by others as well as the overlay to adapt their routing when peers are removed from the network.

The focus of the autonomic capability, however, is at the upper levels of the system model. Agent-based approaches to service orchestration are being investigated as well as methods to enable self-healing to fulfil a given user service requirement in the case of a service failure. These two aspects are related and both rely on the system understanding, to some degree, (a) what the user requirements are, (b) what services are available and how they relate, (c) the expected Quality-of-Service (QoS) services can deliver in a certain context.

Service selection is a key element of a resilient service-oriented middleware providing means to route service requests to the providers which best fit for the task. The problem becomes increasingly difficult in volatile environments where the availability and performance of service providers can change rapidly. In such situations, it is essential that the middleware has the ability to keep track of constant changes and updates its selection procedures accordingly. Decentralised adaptive mechanisms are a promising way in which this can be achieved. In the following section, we describe Mercury adaptive service selection which has been developed as part of the Nexus middleware. The description serves as an example of a concrete implementation of some of the autonomic principles mentioned previously.

3. Autonomic Computing Case Study - Mercury Adaptive Service Selection

3.1. Overview

The Mercury framework [6] is designed for application within an SOA and as such assumes a network of interconnected devices, each capable of hosting a number of processes. The processes may adopt at least one of two roles: service provider or consumer. Service providers offer capabilities that other devices (consumers) can access and use. Mercury-based service-selection takes place on the consumer side and assumes that for every device where there is a service consumer, a selector agent is hosted. Thus in Nexus, we envisage embedding a selector agent at each Nexus node.

Mercury relies on there being some service discovery mechanism in the SOA in order to gain a list of functionally capable service providers for a particular task. This functional discovery is based on those attributes that the service providers advertise in their description and can be provided by other components of Nexus. The Mercury selector agents then use the list of capable services as a basis for further finer-grained, non-functional selection. This is achieved by aggregating QoS data for each of the providers through the consumer's experience of them and ranking them accordingly. The result is a model of selection learnt over time which distinguishes those services which are best at performing the task in terms of the QoS they are expected to deliver.

The QoS data of providers is stored in an instance-based model local to each selector agent and is parameterised by the task, as well as the context. Context is defined as the set of attributes which are external to the task requirements but nevertheless may influence the performance of providers (e.g., performing differently at different times of day). A particular service selector therefore builds up a model of how suited each provider is at fulfilling each particular task in each context.

The main contribution is the design of an efficient distributed service selection framework and (collaborative) algorithms for its construction and real-time adaptation. The learning techniques used are similar to those in reinforcement learning [16], however are novel in the degree to which they are adaptive. Specifically, a decision function is employed (Fig. 2) to ensure that the probability of exploration (selection of services for which there is little or no prior data in the model) is linked to the relative improvement expected when exploration is pursued over exploitation (selection of those for which there is a large amount of data). An adaptive momentum mechanism for updating the model has been developed so that the incorporation of new data into the model is dependent on the amount and recency of the information already stored. The methods used allow a system of multiple agents to be adaptive to changes in the service environment improving the overall QoS of the system, and may be made more effective through introducing collaborative strategies.

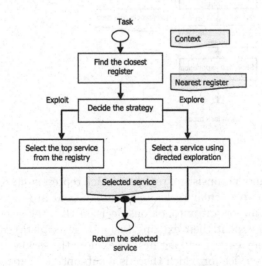

FIGURE 2. Exploration/Exploitation, Decision.

Two collaborative gossiping strategies have been investigated which vary in the degree to which the selector agents share information. The first strategy, anonymous gossiping, involves only partial sharing of information and allows selector agents to gain a better estimation of the distribution of QoS attainable in the network on which the exploration-exploitation control is based. The second collaborative strategy, *full gossiping*, involves sharing detailed information about providers between selectors to speed up learning through exploration. The agents, although cooperative may, however, choose to be selective with the information about providers which they share with others so as not to create unfavourable competition on a subset of service providers, and hence undermine their own performance - *secretive full gossiping*.

The task processing cycle is illustrated in Fig. 3 whereby a task is dispatched to the selector agent and based on both the results of functional service discovery and the selection model built up so far, a service is selected to process the task. The QoS with relation to the task is calculated and used to either *augment* the model if the chosen service was not experienced in the past, or *adapt* the model in the case that there was past experience.

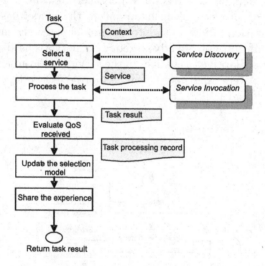

FIGURE 3. Task process cycle.

The selection model consists of registers which represent clusters of experience for services used for particular tasks and contexts and are used to simplify the problem space. An important autonomous decision that the selector agents must make is whether to exploit their existing (usually incomplete) model and choose the service which they expect will act best or explore the service landscape further and either select a service for which there is a sub-optimal expectation of QoS or for which there is no prior experience. In Mercury, the calculation of the expected gain from exploration is distributed by making the agents collaboratively share their expected outcomes. This ensures that agents have a reliable understanding of the distribution of QoS achievable throughout the network of services, improving their decision-making ability of whether to explore or not. Further details of the Mercury framework and similar approaches in literature are discussed in depth in [6]. This includes the defined structure of the model and the precise algorithms involved with its construction and adaptation.

3.2. Related Work

The majority of related work addresses the problem of service selection based on QoS by formalising the QoS requirement space. This is often achieved by defining a QoS ontology [11, 20-22] which is used to specify the qualities that constitute QoS. This is then used for a consumer of a service to specify strict requirements as well as advertising certain quality capabilities from the provider side. Mercury addresses the need for more work dealing with ranking services based on their QoS without explicit QoS requirements as suggested in [19].

The notion of providers advertising their own quality capability, however, brings about the question of trust, which is dealt with by the related works through trust and reputation modelling, in particular [11, 17]. Trust can be used to build relationships between consumers and providers explicitly based on reputation; however the alternative approach taken by Mercury is to build up relationships implicitly based on agent learning dynamics and their interactions with other agents, the details of which make up the main contribution of this work.

A small number of works acknowledge that defining quality requirements and capabilities using precise terms is not always suitable and that instead fuzzy terms of quality may be adopted [4, 20]. It is envisaged that the Mercury framework will be extended to adopt this approach; however, this is left for future work.

In [22], a multidimensional QoS model similar to that of Mercury is presented, although Mercury goes further to propose a mechanism for which this model can be populated in a collaborative fashion using a multi-agent system.

Much of the work surveyed adopts a decentralised (P2P) architecture combining agents to perform collective modelling. Of particular relevance are [3] and [11]: in the former, a reputation model is built based on peer votes for quality; whilst in the latter, quality ratings are shared via rendezvous nodes in the network. Sonnek et al. [15] have developed and evaluated a task allocation mechanism based on statistical modelling of provider reliability. In contrast to our approach, they use a central reputation server, and they do not consider competition between the clients of the allocation mechanism.

We have previously conducted work using a more theoretical approach whereby relationships with service providers are established based on past experience and simple rules which cause emergent self-organisation of peers [14]. Mercury builds on this work by adding task and context-aware capabilities in the internal model of service selection and by introducing the notion of designated selector agents which may collaborate in order to further improve their selection behaviours.

3.3. Experimental Analysis

In order to quantitatively compare the main features of the Mercury framework a simulation environment has been developed which can be populated with n providers of a single service and m service selector agents. We abstract away from the notion of consumers in this case and assume that both the task and context parameters of the problem stay constant.

We were particularly interested in investigating the effectiveness of the system in the case where QoS of a particular service degrades depending on how many simultaneous connections there are to it at any one time. In this sense there is competition for resources and in order to reach an optimal configuration of service selection, it is necessary for the selector agents to both be able to form relationships with certain providers whilst remaining adaptive to changes. In the simulation, the environment is dynamic in the sense that resultant QoS is non-deterministic from an individual selector's point of view due to competition and the distribution of QoS capability can be parameterised.

For all of our experiments the simulation was set up with 30 service providers and 5 selector agents and consumers. The QoS capability distribution was set to uniformly increase such that the 1st provider had the minimum capability and the 30th provider had the maximum (zero and one, respectively). At each time step in the simulation, each selector agent chooses a provider to be invoked and receives the measure of QoS from the provider as a result. The internal selection model is built up through subsequent time steps and at the end of each time step, each selector agent may gossip with other selector agents, depending on their gossiping strategy. The results are averaged over 10 runs.

The first set of experiments was used to compare the different selector agent collaboration strategies on the resultant system (global) QoS attained (Figure 4). It is clear that gossiping enables the QoS to be increased faster and rather unsurprisingly full gossiping produces the fastest rate of QoS increase through the initial stages. The full gossiping approach would be highly effective if at some point the service landscape were to change dramatically. With little or no provider churn, though, full gossiping actually results in a lower QoS than if there was no communication. This demonstrates how, by sharing information about the "best" provider with other agents results in unfavourable competition whereby relationships between a selector S_1 and a particular provider P becomes infected by another selector S_2 which has gained information about P from S_1 and so believes that such a relationship is best for it too. In this case, the global QoS actually decreases. Secretive full gossiping aims to counteract this effect by not sharing "best" providers between selector agents. Indeed, Fig. 4 indicates that the resultant QoS is highest when using the secretive full gossiping strategy. A slight lag compared to the full gossiping curve can be seen and this represents the trade-off of not sharing with other agents the top provider. The secretive full gossiping strategy also clearly performs best in the aggregate performance comparison (Table 1), which takes into account both the resulting level of QoS and the speed with which it is achieved. The anonymous gossiping strategy clearly also proved to be very good but elicits slower convergence which demonstrates that there is a case for sharing direct references to providers such as in the full and secretive strategies. Nevertheless, its effectiveness highlights the importance of collaborating to improve the data on which the exploration/exploitation decision is based.

Collaborative strategy	Aggregate performance
No communication	0.65
Anonymous gossiping	0.69
Full gossiping	0.65
Secretive full gossiping	0.71

TABLE 1. Average aggregate effect of different selector agent collaboration strategies on resultant system QoS derived by averaging each of the 25-cycle sequences.

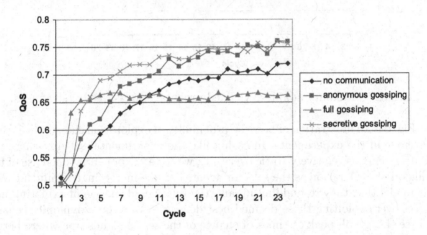

FIGURE 4. Effect of different selector agent collaboration strategies on resultant QoS.

The second set of experiments set out how the adaptive exploration probability mechanism employed by Mercury compared to a fixed strategy. For all the experiments the secretive full gossiping strategy was used although the other strategies produced similar results when tested.

Fig. 5 shows the results from this second experiment set and shows that the adaptive exploration mechanism is particularly useful in the initial stages where little is known about the services available. It also results in a level of QoS almost as good, as the best fixed level of exploration found a value of $\varepsilon = 0.2$ in an ε-greedy strategy [16] resulting in the highest average QoS. The main use of the adaptive exploration, though, is the adaptivity which it gives the system, allowing the selector agents to choose the appropriate amount of exploration given the conditions in the network and the accuracy of their selection models, rather than performing "blindly" following a fixed probability of exploration, or perhaps a pre-defined exploration-exploitation scheduling function.

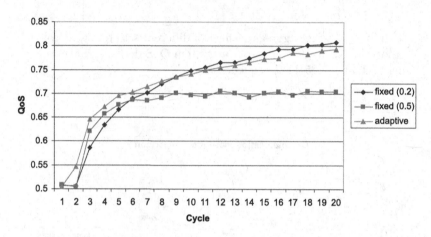

FIGURE 5. Mercury adaptive vs fixed probabilistic (ε-greedy) strategies.

Fig. 6 is an illustration of how the probability of exploration changes over time on average in the experiments. In casing like the experimental set-up, where the QoS data remains relatively static over time, we see an exponential decrease of the likelihood of exploration as the selector agents become increasingly confident with their model that they're building up and the relative advantage of exploring new services over exploiting those deemed best decreases. In a more dynamic scenario we'd see this graph peak at times of change of the service landscape where better services are introduced or perhaps some existing services are able to offer a higher level of QoS. The peaks would signify the selector agents reacting to this change in the service landscape accordingly and the potential for increased exploration would quickly spread throughout the population by means of (anonymous) gossiping.

The Mercury framework is a concrete illustration of how emergent properties can be leveraged to improve global system behaviour in Service-Oriented Architectures, such as Nexus. The combination of local decision-making (exploration/exploitation strategy) with diffusion of QoS information (gossiping) allows a population of selectors with variable needs to collectively identify and converge toward a configuration that meets the requirements of a majority of participants.

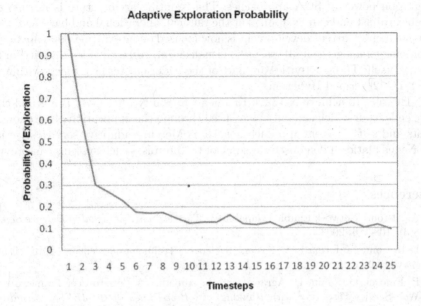

FIGURE 6. Exponential decrease of exploration probability over time as a result of the adaptive mechanism.

Moreover, this distributed problem-solving is largely implicit: the establishment of preferential relationships between selectors and providers incorporates any bias associated with initial conditions and/or the influence of the early history of the system. For instance, in the case that there is competition between two or more selectors for a contended resource, the progressive gain of momentum will ensure that random fluctuations are amplified to the point where only an adequate subset of all competing selectors keep their affiliation with the service. By forcing the 'losers' to identify an alternative provider, this process usually leads to improved global QoS, without any need for central planning or explicit negotiations between selectors.

4. Conclusion

Within the defence domain the problem of data overload continues and will be greatly magnified by the arrival of new high bandwidth sensor arrays and persistent surveillance systems. In addition the lack of skilled IT support manpower makes the problem particularly acute in the defence sector. The Nexus platform is an attempt to merge the best of autonomic computing and agent-based techniques to create a self-organising and self-healing service delivery capability. The result combines the resilience of P2P networks with the service management and legacy integration power of SOA approaches. The resulting architecture is intrinsically scalable, robust and can be applied at the tactical, operational and back-end layers of deployment. Current development is now focused on integrating new capabilities for ontology management, 3D scenario visualisation, and embedded security for the network itself. These activities are part of the wider cluster of projects within the DIF DTC [2] termed Hyperion.

The race to achieve Network Enabled Capability (or NCW) is a grand challenge endeavour which can only be realised through the application of autonomous agents and self-* system approaches, such as Mercury adaptive service selection. The Nexus platform demonstrates some of the promises such systems can provide.

References

[1] A. Alston, "Network Enabled Capability - The Concept," *Journal of Defence Science* 8(3), 108-116, 2003.

[2] Data and Information Fusion Defence Technology Centre (DIF DTC), www.difdtc.com

[3] F. Emekci, O. Sahin, D. Agrawal and A. Abbadi, "A Peer-to-Peer Framework for Web Service Discovery with Ranking," in *Proceedings of the IEEE International Conference on Web Service (ICWS'04)*, Washington DC, USA, 2004, p. 192.

[4] C.- L. Huang, C.- C Lo, Y. Li, K.- M Chao, J.- Y Chung and Y. Huang, "Service Discovery through Multi-Agent Consensus," in *Proc. of IEEE Int. Workshop on Service-Oriented System Engineering (SOSE'05)*, pp. 37-44, 2005.

[5] M. N. Huhns, M. P. Singh, "Service-Oriented Computing: Key Concepts and Principles," *IEEE Internet Computing* 9(1), pp. 75-81, 2005.

[6] M. Jakob, A. Healing, F. Saffre, "Mercury: Multi-Agent Adaptive Service Selection Based on Non-Functional Attributes," to appear in *Proc. of the 2nd International Workshop on Engineering Emergence in Decentralised Autonomic Systems,*

[7] M. Jakob, N. Kaveh and R. A. Ghanea-Hercock, "Nexus - Middleware for Decentralized Service-Oriented Information Fusion," in *Proc. of Specialists' Meeting on Information Fusion for Command Support*, The Hague, Nov 2005.

[8] Java Message Service, http://java.sun.com/products/jms/

[9] N. Kaveh, R. Ghanea-Hercock, "NEXUS: Resilient Intelligent Middleware," *BT Technology Journal*, 22(3), pp. 209-215, 2004.

[10] J. O. Kephart and D. M. Chess, "The vision of autonomic computing," *IEEE Computer*, 36(1), pp. 41-50, 2003.

[11] E. M. Maximillen and M. P. Singh, "Multiagent System for Dynamic Web Services Selection," in *Proc. of the AAMAS Workshop on Service-Oriented Computing and Agent-Based Engineering (SOCABE)*, Utrecht, July 2005.

[12] R. Mondejar et al., "Towards a Decentralized p2pWeb Service Oriented Architecture," in *Proc. of 2nd Int. Workshop on Collaborative P2P Information Systems (COPS 2006)*, Manchester, UK, 2006.

[13] M. Paolucci and K. Sycara, "Autonomous Semantic Web Services," *IEEE Internet Computing*, 7(5):34-41, 2003.

[14] F. Saffre and H. R. Blok, "SelfService: A theoretical protocol for autonomic distribution of services in P2P communities," in *Proc. of 12th IEEE International Conference and Workshops on the Engineering of Computer-Based Systems*, Maryland, April 2005, pp. 528-534.

[15] J. Sonnek, M. Nathan, A. Chandra and J. Weissman, "Reputation-Based Scheduling on Unreliable Distributed Infrastructures," in *Proc. of the 26th IEEE International Conference on Distributed Computing Systems (ICDCS'06)*, 2006.

[16] R. S. Sutton and A. G. Barto, *Reinforcement Learning: An Introduction*. Cambridge, MA: MIT Press, 1998.

[17] W.T. Teacy, J. Patel, N.R. Jennings and M. Luck, "Travos: Trust and reputation in the context of inaccurate information sources," *Autonomous Agents and Multi-Agent Systems*, 12(2), 2006.

[18] P. Van Roy, A. Ghodsi, S. Haridi, J.- B. Stefani, T. Coupaye, A. Reinefeld, E. Winter, R. Yap, "Self Management of Large-Scale Distributed Systems by Combining Peer-to-Peer Networks and Components," *CoreGRID Technical Report*, TR-0018, 2005.

[19] L.- H. Vu, M. Hauswirth and K. Aberer, "Towards P2P-based Semantic Web Service Discovery with QoS Support," in *Proc. of Workshop on Business Processes and Services (BPS)*, Nancy, France, 2005.

[20] P. Wang, K.- M Chao, C.- C Lo, C.- L Huang and Y. Li, "A Fuzzy Model for Selection of QoS-Aware Web Services," in *Proc. of IEEE International Conference on e-Business Engineering (ICEBE'06)*, 2006.

[21] X. Wang, T. Vitvar, M. Kerrigan, I. Toma, "Synthetical Evaluation of Multiple Qualities for Service Selection," in *Proc. of the 4th International Conference on Service Oriented Computing*, Springer-Verlag LNCS series, Chicago, USA, December, 2006.

[22] L. Zeng, B. Benatallah, A. H. H. Ngu, M. Dumas, J. Kalagnanam, and H. Chang, "QoS-Aware Middleware for Web Services Composition," *IEEE Transactions on Software Engineering*, 30(5), May 2004.

Alex Healing, Robert Ghanea-Hercock and Hakan Duman
Pervasive ICT Research Centre
British Telecom, United Kingdom
e-mail: `alex.healing@bt.com`
     `robert.ghanea-hercock@bt.com`
     `hakan.duman@bt.com`

Michal Jakob
Gerstner Laboratory
Czech Technical University
Czech Republic
e-mail: `jakob@labe.felk.cvut.cz`

Whitestein Series in Software Agent Technologies, 15–32
© 2007 Birkhäuser Verlag Basel/Switzerland

Information-Based Control of Decentralised Sensor Networks

David Nicholson, Sarvapali D. Ramchurn and Alex Rogers

Abstract. This chapter describes how formal information measures can be used as the basis for enabling decentralised, intelligent and autonomous control of large-scale sensor network resources, with widespread application throughout the military and security domain. These information measures are the result of filtering and fusing local sensor observations, assimilating the products over a communication network, and interpreting them in the wider context to infer underlying states of interest to the military or security operation. Information provides a currency against which a constrained set of sensing and communication actions can be valued, resulting in a single action or sequence of actions being executed. This is known as Information-Based Control (IBC). The main focus of this chapter is the problem of *decentralised* IBC in a large-scale sensor network, and its solution in terms of multi-agent system methodologies. Examples and applications, relevant to the military world, are used to highlight a number of important practical considerations.

1. Introduction

Over the last decade military doctrine has been shifting to reflect the widespread view that *decentralised* data and information systems are key to achieving (and sustaining) the required level of operational tempo to defeat agile adversaries. Decentralised systems are characterised by horizontal information exchanges and coordination processes between peers. They are expected to be more flexible, scalable, and robust than single monolithic systems [1].

In addition to increased decentralisation of military systems and processes, there is also an impetus to increase their level of intelligent autonomy. This could range from smart sensors that automatically adapt their update rate, to communication networks that self-organise and adaptively route messages, through to platforms that plan their own trajectories. The DARPA Grand Challenge has promoted rapid development in this last area [2].

The imperative in most military operations is to rapidly seek, extract, store, and recover, relevant information in support of operational objectives. In a decentralised sensor network (DSN), multiple processes will be running asynchronously and interacting over a network. It is vital that these interactions are managed and controlled, otherwise they may conflict with one another, leading to poor performance. This motivates the need for some form of decentralised intelligent control mechanism that can automate the system, whilst also maintaining scalability and flexibility.

The multi-agent system paradigm is a natural one for modelling and controlling such decentralised systems. In this context, individual decision nodes within the sensor network can be conceived as autonomous intelligent agents, each with their own capabilities, constraints and goals. Such agents have to make decisions such as, *how, what and when to sense*, or *what, when and with whom to communicate*, given constraints such as limited bandwidth or computational resources. A principled measure of information provides a common metric that the agents seek to maximise through their individual sensing and communication decisions. This leads to an approach that we term information-based control (IBC).

This chapter provides a general formulation of the IBC problem (Section 2) before relating it specifically to DSN systems and identifying some solutions (Section 3). Then a number of examples and applications are provided to highlight various implementation details and practical issues (Section 4). The chapter closes with some discussion of the key points and conclusions (Section 5).

1.1. Background

The main content of this chapter is drawn from recent projects in which one of the authors (employed by BAE Systems Advanced Technology Centre) has been involved. These projects were undertaken in collaboration with several BAE Systems university partners and fall in the general subject area of decentralised data and information systems. The specific projects represented here are as follows:

- ANSER [3]: This project formulated the mathematical basis for distributed data fusion (DDF) in large-scale sensor networks, developed practical algorithms for DDF, and demonstrated DDF in the real world by implementing it on board multiple airborne platforms. The project was funded by BAE Systems and performed by the University of Sydney (Australian Centre for Field Robotics).

- ARGUS [4]: This project is developing a foundation for decentralised integration of multiple autonomous fusion agents by exploiting synergies between machine learning and multi-agent systems. The fundamental research is being carried out at two universities (Oxford and Southampton) and matured into three distinct industrial demonstrators (by BAE Systems, Rolls Royce and QinetiQ). The project is funded by the MOD, EPSRC and DTI, as well as by the industrial partners themselves.

- RCSC(18B) [5]: This project developed decentralised IBC algorithms for target identification and localisation and carried out a number of field trials with multiple UAV platforms to demonstrate some of these algorithms. The work was performed in collaboration with the University of Sydney (Australian Centre for Field Robotics). The project was funded by the UK's MOD.

- SEAS AA011 [12]: This project is developing methods for decentralised adaptive control and exploring various practical issues associated with coordination and cooperation. The work is funded by the Systems Engineering and Autonomous Systems (SEAS) Defence Technology Centre established by the UK MOD.
- SEAS AA009 [6]: This project is developing architectures and algorithms for adaptive (reactive and proactive) data gathering and dissemination in autonomous sensor networks. The work is funded by the Systems Engineering and Autonomous Systems (SEAS) Defence Technology Centre established by the UK MOD.
- ALADDIN [8]: This project is developing mechanisms, architectures, and techniques to deal with the dynamic and uncertain nature of decentralised intelligent systems in the application context of disaster management. This application has military and security parallels with urban operations, such as curfew keeping and patrol and search/rescue of hostages. The project is funded by BAE Systems and EPSRC.

1.2. Related Work

Intelligent control of decentralised sensor networks has been the subject of vigorous research over recent years, much of it stimulated by the challenging problems raised by military and security applications. The research is being pursued by a range of communities (e.g., statistics, signal processing, computer science, data fusion, artificial intelligence) and many of its novel results are the direct outcome of a cross-disciplinary approach.

The information-theoretic bridge between sensor fusion and sensor management has now been developed in detail [14, 15] and has been applied in the context of military target detection, identification and tracking [17]. More recently, principled information-theoretic approaches have also been applied to the design of wireless sensor networks in order to facilitate intelligent sensing and sampling decisions when communication and sensor battery life are severely constrained [16].

However, classical estimation and information theory is not ideally suited to deal with the organisational complexities of large-scale sensor networks. Consequently, this issue has attracted new perspectives and contributions from the fields of artificial intelligence and multi-agent systems. Work in this area seeks to combine principled information metrics with agent-based negotiation and coordination algorithms, and progress to date includes the application of distributed multi-agent negotiation algorithms to the problem of combinatorial task allocation within sensor networks [18], the use of concepts such as coalition formation to describe and solve sensor tasking problems [19], and the application of novel market-based approaches for decentralised control [20].

2. Information-Based Control

This section formulates the IBC problem for a single smart sensor node, or agent. The agent can intelligently control how, where and/or when it observes the world, by automatically selecting for itself an action, $\mathbf{a}$, i.e., in general a vector of instantaneous or time-extended, discrete, continuous or mixed-type control variables.

This process requires the agent to rate all its possible actions with respect to some measure of utility $U(\mathbf{a}, \mathbf{x})$, where $\mathbf{x}$ is the true state of the world. Due to uncertainty, the agent will only have access to probabilistic knowledge of $\mathbf{x}$, denoted by $P(\mathbf{x}|\mathbf{Z}^n)$, where $\mathbf{Z}^n$ refers to a set of N observations of the state, $\{\mathbf{z}_1, \dots, \mathbf{z}_N\}$. In practice, the agent can calculate $P(\mathbf{x}|\mathbf{Z}^n)$ in recursive fashion, following each observation, by means of a suitable Bayes filtering and fusion algorithm [9].

Clearly, because $\mathbf{x}$ is not exactly known, neither is $U(\mathbf{a}, \mathbf{x})$. It is therefore more meaningful to define an expected utility, following an action $\mathbf{a}$, as follows (replacing the integral with a summation for discrete states):

$$\bar{U}(\mathbf{a}) = \int_{\mathbf{x}} U(\mathbf{x}, \mathbf{a}) P(\mathbf{x}|\mathbf{Z}^n) d\mathbf{x} \qquad (2.1)$$

Bayesian Decision Theory (BDT) offers a powerful framework for making decisions under uncertainty [10]. According to BDT, the Bayes action is the strategy that maximises the expected utility,

$$\mathbf{a}^* = \arg\max_{\mathbf{a}} \bar{U}(\mathbf{a}) \qquad (2.2)$$

All that is now needed to construct a theoretical framework for IBC is a definition of $U(\mathbf{x}, \mathbf{a})$. For a sensor agent a good definition is the log likelihood given by,

$$U(\mathbf{x}, \mathbf{a}) = \log P(\mathbf{x}|\mathbf{a}) \qquad (2.3)$$

This is the logarithm of the posterior probability density (or mass) function for each of the agent's possible actions. Formally, this choice for $U(\mathbf{x}, \mathbf{a})$ satisfies what is known as the 'rationality axioms' and induces a preference structure on the action space in the form of an ordered set [10]. Moreover, the expected value of this quantity turns out to be (negative) entropy or Shannon Information.

It is now clear how information-based control arises from BDT. The sensor agent is filtering its observations and controlling how, where and/or when, it acquires subsequent observations, on the basis of the information these observations are expected to generate. The Bayes action, defined by (2.2), is the action that maximises this information. If the action is to acquire further observations, then IBC is effectively a closed loop process of sensing, filtering/fusing, deciding and acting.

As an example, suppose a sensing agent is engaged in tracking a target with a standard state estimator, the Kalman filter. Based on observations made up to and including time k, a type of information associated with its estimate is quantified by the inverse error covariance, $\mathbf{Y}_\mathbf{a}(k|k) \equiv \mathbf{P}_\mathbf{a}^{-1}(k|k)$. This is known as Fisher information. It depends on the control action taken by the sensor prior to its observation (e.g., an adjustment to its zoom, frequency range, or detection threshold parameter, depending on the type of the sensor). The entropic information associated with the estimate is given by,

$$H(k) = \frac{1}{2} \log \left[(2\pi e)^n |\mathbf{Y}_{\mathrm{a}}(k|k)| \right] \tag{2.4}$$

There are a variety of practical methods for calculating $\mathbf{a}$. If $\mathbf{a}$ is discrete and low-dimensional, the IBC problem could be solved simply by direct search. If $\mathbf{a}$ is smooth, continuous and differentiable, it could be solved by a gradient descent method (e.g., Sequential Quadratic Programming). Alternatively, Simulated Annealing or Genetic Algorithms may be more suitable for non-smooth, discontinuous functions.

For some problems it may be advantageous to optimise a time sequence of future actions rather than simply the next action. Such non-myopic sensing policies can be implemented by dynamic programming methods, but the computational cost of these methods is typically very high.

3. Decentralised Sensor Networks

This section considers the extension of IBC to decentralised sensor networks, in which there are now multiple sensor agents communicating over a network. The individual sensing actions are as before, what, where, and when to sense, but now there are additional communication actions, such as *request X from node A* and *send Y to node B*. Furthermore, since there are multiple agents (which may be sensors, vehicles, or human assets in the military context) there may also be multiple conflicting objectives that need to be managed in addition to a single overarching goal for the entire system. Problems of this nature are often formulated and solved in terms of game theory [20].

The cooperative (or team) game problem is considered below. In this problem the local sensing and communication actions are all selflessly directed toward optimising the global system-wide goal which is known to each agent. To further simplify matters, the agents all agree up front on a formal information measure (Fisher, Shannon, or Mutual Information) of the quality of their decisions.

A simple extension of IBC for a single sensor, to a multi-sensor system, is for each sensor node to calculate an optimal action with respect to a local utility $U(\mathbf{x}, \mathbf{a})$. In general this would result in actions that could 'clash' or conflict, leading to poor performance or even dangerous behaviours (e.g., two UAVs trying to occupy the same region of airspace). Consequently, some sort of iterative gaming process is required, whereby the agents repeatedly interact and negotiate over potential solutions until the process (hopefully) equilibrates on the optimal joint action for the system.

In single sensor IBC, the $\mathbf{x}$ component of $U(\mathbf{x}, \mathbf{a})$ was calculated by an estimation algorithm such as the Kalman filter. In decentralised sensor networks, $\mathbf{x}$ (and the estimation error covariance $\mathbf{P}$) is calculated by a decentralised estimation process. By transforming the estimation variables, $\mathbf{Y} \equiv \mathbf{P}^{-1}$ and $\mathbf{y} \equiv \mathbf{P}^{-1}\mathbf{x}$, a remarkably simple equation for fusing estimates from node i and node j at time k arises:

$$\mathbf{y}_{i \cup j}(k|k) = \mathbf{y}_i(k|k) + \mathbf{y}_j(k|k) - \mathbf{y}_{i \cap j}(k|k) \tag{3.1}$$

$$\mathbf{Y}_{i \cup j}(k|k) = \mathbf{Y}_i(k|k) + \mathbf{Y}_j(k|k) - \mathbf{Y}_{i \cap j}(k|k) \tag{3.2}$$

The key to implementing these equations is calculating the common information terms $\mathbf{y}_{i \cap j}(k|k)$ and $\mathbf{Y}_{i \cap j}(k|k)$. This can be done exactly for fully-connected and singly-connected (tree) networks [21], and covariance intersection provides a provably conservative estimate in large-scale sensor networks [22].

The information fusion products generated by decentralised estimation offer a principled currency for the iterative negotiation process that underpins decentralised IBC. There are several ways to implement this process in practice, but the overarching requirement is to avoid mass exchange of every sensor node's expected utilities. For IBC problems that are smooth and continuous, this can be achieved by decentralised gradient descent algorithms [23]. For IBC problems with discrete control variables, the nodes could form a utility-ranked list of their actions and only communicate the top few actions. An important practical consideration is the structure of the global utility function. If this is separable, or even partially separable, it can lead to efficient decentralised IBC algorithms, such as the sum-product algorithm for discrete actions [25] and related information aggregation methods for continuous actions [24].

4. Examples and Applications

This section describes some specific examples of decentralised IBC.

4.1. Platform Control

In this example, which formed part of the RCSC(18B) project (see Section 1.1 for details), a colour vision camera was installed on two UAV platforms and they were flown against a number of artificial (stationary) ground targets. The mission was to localise all of the targets to a pre-specified level of accuracy. This was formulated as a decentralised task assignment problem. Each UAV calculated the following utility function associated with observing each target,

$$J = \frac{MI\left([\mathbf{y}, \mathbf{Y}], \mathbf{a}\right)}{T} \tag{4.1}$$

which is the mutual information gain divided by the time taken for it to be reached.

This information-based utility function enables each UAV to preference order its targets and decide which is the best target to visit and observe next. A global utility function is defined as the sum of individual local utilities for each combination of target assignments.

By sharing their local utility values, each UAV is able to implement a simple assignment algorithm to determine the optimal assignment that maximises the global utility function. The planning of the UAVs was synchronised using GPS. At uniform intervals the UAVs calculate and communicate their local utility values and re-evaluate their target assignment. If the target assignment has changed they replan a path to the new target. If not, they remain on path to observe their current target. The UAVs are also communicating their observations throughout the mission, so they have up-to-date information on which to make decisions.

The mission comprised 14 minutes of flight time during which the UAVs planned paths to 13 separate targets in their surveillance volume. They were able to cooperate for most of this time, communicating and sharing information until the mission was completed. The typical paths of the two UAVs are shown in Fig. 1, which is split into six time segments. The UAVs initially start from a loiter pattern (top left). The general behaviour of the team is (as expected) to maintain high average target information. Once a target has been observed for a while it becomes more beneficial to switch to another which has much less information. Thus the targets to the left which are initially observed are revisited later on when the information about the other targets has been raised. Also it can be seen that the UAVs generally choose targets that are nearby due to the weighted utility function.

Fig. 2 plots the Shannon information for each target, held by one of the UAVs, as a function of the mission time. It can be seen how those targets with low initial information (high uncertainty) are observed first until their information is increased to a level comparable with the rest of the targets.

4.2. Sensor Control

The next example, based on work carried out under the SEAS DTC project AA011 (see Section 1.1 for details), highlights a powerful new framework for decentralised adaptive control known as Probability Collectives (PC) [11]. In terms of multi-agent systems, PC can be viewed as a system of bounded rational agents playing an iterative game. The example considers a surveillance and tracking problem in which multiple (stationary) sensors are observing multiple (mobile) targets. Each sensor can only observe a single target at each time step, although multiple sensors may view the same target. Consequently, the discrete joint action space in this case is the set of all possible sensor-to-target assignments.

The specific test scenario is illustrated in Fig. 3. There are three networked sensor nodes and three targets. The targets move at constant speed in the directions shown and the sensor nodes track them with decentralised Kalman filters (DKFs). In order to develop the target track estimates from time k to $k + 1$, each node does the following:

1. Projects its DKFs by one time step
2. Chooses a target to observe next
3. Observes its chosen target
4. Updates its DKFs with local observations
5. Updates its DKFs with communicated observations
6. Returns to step 1 and repeats

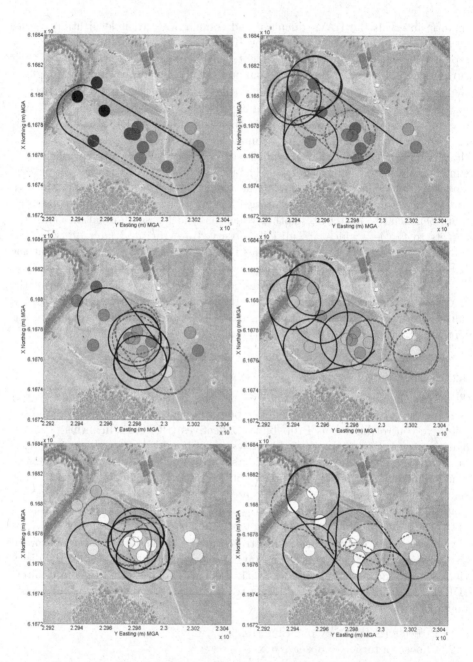

FIGURE 1. The resulting paths of each UAV during the decentralised IBC mission (UAV 1 - bold line; UAV 2 - dashed line). The plot is divided into time segments from left to right, top to bottom. Also shown are the 13 targets which the UAVs are tasked with localising. The shaded circles show how much information the UAVs have about each target (black is zero and white indicates the information threshold has been met).

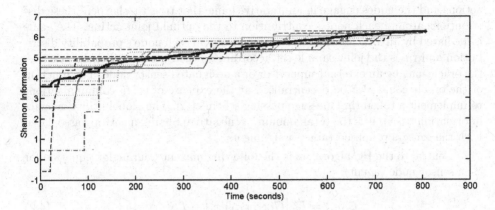

FIGURE 2. The Shannon information for each of the 13 targets, calculated by one of the flight vehicles, as a function of the mission time. The solid black line represents the average Shannon information for all the targets.

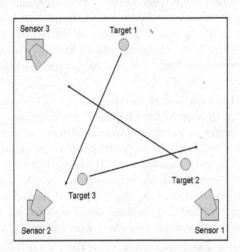

FIGURE 3. Multi-sensor, multi-target tracking scenario. Each sensor can only observe one target at a time and it has to decide which one.

Applying the PC framework to sensor control, step 2 above can be decentralised, avoiding mass exchange of utility functions between each sensor node. Instead, each node maintains a probability distribution over its discrete control actions and the nodes engage in an iterative game that tries to 'sharpen' these distributions around each node's contribution to the optimal joint action. The game is mediated by an 'oracle' who receives samples from each node's probability distribution and rates the joint sample set according to their global utility. In practice, the oracle may be an external supervisor or a designated sensor node. The function of the oracle could also be decentralised at the expense of extra communications to implement a token ring message passing scheme [12]. The global utility is again information based: it is the total amount of (negative) Shannon entropy associated with the sensors proposed target assignments.

Central to the PC algorithm is the following maxent Lagrangian equation for each sensor node (agent):

$$\mathcal{L}_i(q_i) = E_q\left[G(x_i, x_{\{i\}})|x_i\right] - TS(q_i) \tag{4.2}$$

where x_i is the sensor's discrete set of actions, $x_{\{i\}}$ denotes the set of all sensors other than sensor i, q_i is the probability distribution on the sensor's action space, $S(q_i)$ is the entropy associated with that distribution, $G(x)$ is the global utility function and T can be viewed as a temperature variable.

The algorithm involves each agent Monte-Carlo sampling from q_i, communicating those samples to the oracle, and descending its maxent Lagrangian function in response to feedback from the oracle. T is lowered during this process, according to some fixed schedule, until the updated probability distributions converge. At this point the actions corresponding to the mean (or median) of their probability distributions are executed by the sensors.

Now returning to the example, the performance of PC was compared against a baseline and a benchmark algorithm. The baseline algorithm was simply to have each sensor choose its target at random. This algorithm was not expected to perform well since there is no notion of coordination or cooperation whatsoever. The benchmark algorithm has each sensor selfishly choosing the target which maximises its own predicted (negative) Shannon entropy, while completely ignoring the preference of the other sensors. This algorithm is expected to perform reasonably because of implicit coordination in the sensors actions due to the underlying DKF processes which tend to synchronise their world view.

The actual results of a simulation based on the scenario shown in Fig. 3 are displayed in Fig. 4. As expected, the *Random* sensor-to-target assignment strategy is always outperformed by *PC* and the *Selfish* assignment strategies. *PC* also outperforms *Selfish* during the middle phase of the scenario. This is because the targets are then roughly equidistant from the sensors and their observations carry comparable value. Consequently, the *Selfish* strategy results in somewhat chaotic, near-random assignments, whereas the fully cooperative PC algorithm produces a smooth and emergent switch in sensor-to-target assignments. This switching behaviour was also observed in the optimal centralised solution, which the *PC* solution effectively traced throughout the entire scenario.

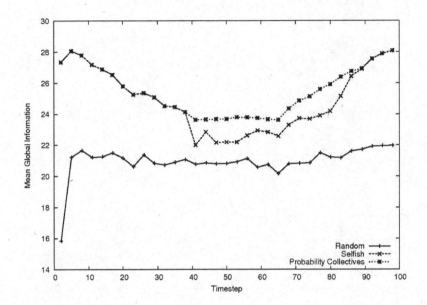

FIGURE 4. The sensor nodes average information plotted as a function of time for the Random (full line), Selfish (dashed line) and PC (dotted line) sensor-to-target assignment algorithms.

4.3. Communication Control

This example considers active information flow in decentralised sensor networks. This refers to smart dissemination of information over a network, with due regard to the local utilities of receiver/sender nodes or the global utility of the system, as well as communication resource constraints. It may be possible to organise such flows on the basis of simple rules or heuristics, but these often require careful 'hand-tuning' and are unlikely to offer much flexibility.

A more general approach, developed under the SEAS DTC project AA009 (see Section 1.1 for details), is highlighted in this section. A typical motivating problem is shown in Fig. 5. This is a surveillance mission scenario, involving multiple decentralised and heterogenous agents and users, operating in an uncertain and hostile environment, where communications are limited. The problem is what information should the agents and users exchange to ensure timely execution of their mission goal(s)?

There are two variants of IBC that can be applied to this problem. Both are underpinned by Bayesian Decision Theory but differ in their implementation details depending on whether the sensor nodes have a common objective or unequal

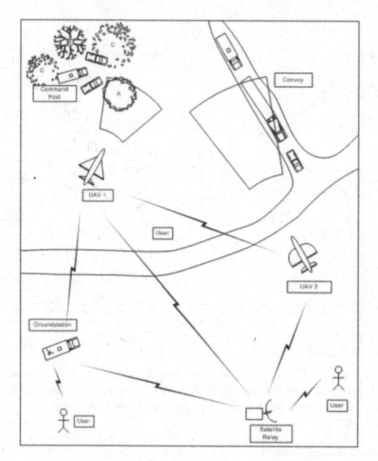

FIGURE 5. Surveillance scenario involving multiple sensing agents
and multiple users. Of interest is how the agents and users should
interact to gather relevant data in a rapid and effective manner.

objectives. Each variant was evaluated in simulation against a target identification
problem (represented by a Bayesian Network). In each case there was an emphasis on providing scalable decentralised solutions. This ruled out the conceptually
simple approach of replicating the centralised solution at each node, because that
requires each sensor node to acquire all the other sensor nodes expected utilities.

The first method, developed for common local utility functions, is characterised by information *push* in reaction to what is known by a transmitting node
about a receiving node's information requirements [6]. Two smart steps are required to implement this method:

1. The probabilistic world model is represented in a compact factored form
   known as a junction tree. This enables an algorithm for inference *within*

Bayesian Networks to also perform inference *between* Bayesian Networks at separate locations.
2. An efficient communication protocol is used to minimise inconsistencies between the probabilistic estimates of state maintained by each node. Specifically, Kullback-Leibler divergence is used to monitor and prioritise information flow in the system.

The main strength of this method is its efficiency: it uses fewer resources than competing methods when resources are unconstrained, and provides faster convergence and increased accuracy when communication is constrained. However, the intrinsic weakness of this method is its assumption of a common objective. In military operations, it is quite likely that sensor nodes will have different objectives which are related to their local context. Moreover, each node's local objective is unlikely to be known to the other nodes.

The second method, developed for different objective functions, is characterised by information *pull*, which is a proactive advertisement by the sensor nodes for information that supports their local objectives [7]. As in the information push scheme, two smart steps are required to implement this method:

1. A means of generating advertisements that can be interpreted by receiving agents and used as a basis for information gathering and communication decisions. A suitable advertisement is a vector containing the average utility change for every possible request, normalised to form a set of priorities over actions.
2. An efficient "in-network" scheme for aggregating advertisements and information. By using a tree communication topology and storing the advertisements received on each link, it is possible to formulate and propagate an aggregated advertisement. In this way agents can use "link demands" to steer information toward the desired destinations.

In common with the information push method this method is also scalable because it communicates and fuses estimates rather than sensor data, it exploits structure in the world model, and it prevents stale data from being re-transmitted. In exchange for its scalability and flexibility with respect to multiple objectives, the information pull method trades optimality in performance.

These concepts for communication control were exposed to a simple experiment in which five (simulated) airborne sensor nodes were tasked with maintaining surveillance of targets in their own areas of interest and reflecting this self-interest in their private utility functions. The sensor nodes are ignorant about each other's utilities. Within the scenario there are three sensor types. Each sensor can distinguish different target attributes, but evidence from all three sensors is required to positively identify a specific target type. The performance of each sensor is captured using a naive Bayes classifier.

The experiment compares performance for the information push/pull approaches in terms of the Shannon information utility averaged over nodes. The

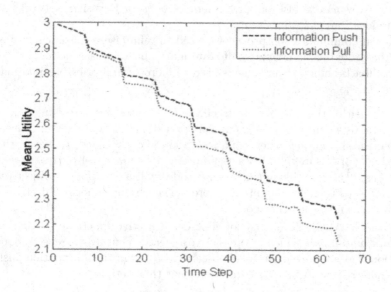

FIGURE 6. The mean Shannon information utility for a bandwidth-limited sensor network implementing information push and pull algorithms as shown. Information pull performs better (i.e., has lower Shannon information) due to the differing objectives of the sensor agents

results are shown in Fig. 6. The information push approach assumes common objectives and in this scenario, where the sensors have their own private interests that are unknown to other sensors, it is outperformed by the more flexible information pull approach.

4.4. Complex System Control

To conclude this section it is useful to consider complex systems composed of multiple agents, each with their own aims, objectives, and constraints that either cooperate or must be incentivised to interact so as to achieve the systems designers' goals. In such systems, it is important to balance sensing actions against other decisions (e.g., to communicate or act on the variables in the environment) since every action taken may have an impact on the achievement of system-wide objectives. Such issues typically arise in the real world in the form of major events, such as large scale disasters. Disaster management forms the application focus for a recently initiated project known as ALADDIN (see Section 1.1 for details).

The main aim of ALADDIN is to develop methods and architectures for modelling, designing, and building *decentralised systems* that will cope with uncertain and biased information (e.g., due to defective sensors, inaccuracies in measurements), unreliable communication (e.g., network nodes breakdown, noisy channels), and multiple agents that may belong to different stakeholders (e.g., fire brigades, local government, ambulances). In so doing, the ALADDIN project aims to provide strong, both theoretical and practical, foundations for Disaster Management (DM) systems that are characterised by a diverse set of resources which need to support multiple users with different priorities and time horizons. This requires a flexible framework (architecture and algorithms) for addressing dynamic decentralised resource allocation problems. In the ALADDIN project this requirement is being met by cross-fertilising ideas from machine learning, information fusion, and multi-agent systems.

This powerful combination provides methods for managing uncertain data and executing single actor IBC as well as methods for decentralised coordination and control of multiple actors. Thus, machine learning and information fusion algorithms will generally aim to transform multiple streams of corrupted data into information which can then be used to action sensors, vehicles or rescuers, within the DM system. Building upon this, multi-agent systems techniques will aim to facilitate decentralised resource allocation in various ways ranging from market-based control, through coalition formation, to distributed constraints optimisation techniques.

To ensure that theoretical results from research in these areas connects to the real-world problem of disaster management, the ALADDIN project is building its own experimental testbeds and using existing ones, such as the RoboCup Rescue simulation testbed [13]. In particular, Robocup Rescue has been identified as a compelling environment for demonstrating the ALADDIN technologies, since it hosts many of the issues that the project is trying to tackle: uncertainty, bias, and multi-agency. Moreover, sensors with any specific property or capability can be modelled in the environment in such a way that they impact on the decision making process of individual or multiple agents. Such a testbed will therefore be useful for demonstrating and evaluating IBC solutions. An example of a 3-D map used by the RoboCup Rescue simulator is shown in Fig. 7 [26].

5. Discussion and Conclusions

Decentralised sensor networks are expected to be a cornerstone of future defence and security systems. They will need to operate over large areas, for long periods of time, with minimal human supervision. Some of the sensors will be stationary and placed at fixed locations in the area of interest; other sensors will be mobile and can visit multiple locations. The sensors may communicate, but the network topology is unlikely to be fixed or known, and the communication bandwidth will be limited. The operational modes of the sensors, their trajectories through the environment, and the information they exchange, are all control variables that may self-adapt to the local goals of individual sensors or to the global goal of the system

FIGURE 7. 3-D map used by the RoboCup Rescue simulator

at large. This is a control problem and it was described how formal measures of information provide a meaningful control basis in decentralised sensor networks.

The multi-agent systems methodology provides a framework and associated tools and techniques for enabling decentralised IBC in sensor networks. While statistics and sensor fusion are equipped with methods to manage uncertainty in these systems, and simple IBC methods can be used to control separate sensors, neither is able to promote the large-scale coordination that is required to maximise the performance of the full decentralised sensor network. However, multi-agent systems methods can usefully fill this gap and help design systems that must consider complex trade-offs in their decision-making. These methods are typically decentralised and deal with dynamism as well as a multiplicity of objectives, further increasing their appeal in the military and security domain.

This exciting field of research needs to develop in several ways. Theoretically, it would be useful to develop a system-level understanding and analysis of cooperative feedback between networked sensor nodes. This would identify the key characteristics of networked sensing problems that benefit from cooperative solutions as well as quantifying the degree of cooperation that is required. Algorithmically, the focus should be on developing practical algorithms that are flexible and scalable in domains where there is dynamism, uncertainty of various forms, and stringent physical resource constraints. Finally, in terms of applications, agent-based optimisation methods may offer novel perspectives on many other long-standing problems in networked sensor fusion systems, including sensor registration, data association, routing topologies for information products, rumour propagation, and decentralised situation assessment.

References

[1] D.S. Alberts, J.J. Garstka, and F.P. Stein, *Network Centric Warfare: Developing and Leveraging Information Superiority*. 2nd Edition, Washington DC, CCRP Press, 2002. (Available online at www.dodccrp.org/publicat.htm)

[2] www.darpa.mil/grandchallenge

[3] S. Sukkarieh, E. Nettleton, J-H. Kim, M. Ridley, A. Göktoğan and H.F. Durrant-Whyte, "The ANSER project: data fusion across multiple uninhabited air vehicles," *Intl. Journal of Robotics Research*, **22:7/8**, pp.505-540, 2003.

[4] www.robots.ox.ac/~argus

[5] D. Cole, S. Sukkarieh and A. Göktoğan, "System development and demonstration of a UAV control architecture for information gathering missions," *Journal of Field Robotics*, **23:6/7**, pp. 417-440, 2006.

[6] P. Bladon and P. Day, "Reactive data gathering", in *Proc. of 1st SEAS DTC Technical Conference*, Edinburgh, 2006. (Available online at www.seasdtc.com/events/algor_and_arch.htm)

[7] P. Bladon, G. Hester, C. Lloyd, D. Nicholson and M. Williams, "Proactive data gathering," in *Proc. of 2nd SEAS DTC Technical Conference*, Edinburgh, 2007.

[8] www.aladdinproject.org

[9] B. Ristic, S. Arulampalam, and N. Gordon, *Beyond the Kalman Filter: Particle Filters for Tracking Applications*. Artech House, 2004.

[10] J.O. Berger, *Statistical Decision Theory and Bayesian Analysis*. Springer Verlag, 1985.

[11] D.H. Wolpert and S. Bieniawski, "Distributed control by Lagrangian steepest descent," in *Proc. of the IEEE Control and Decision Conf.*, pp. 1562-1567, 2004.

[12] A. Waldock and D. Nicholson, "Cooperative decentralised data fusion using Probability Collectives," in *Proc. 1st International Workshop on Agent Technology for Sensor Networks (ATSN-07)*, Hawaii, 2007. (Available online at userc.ecs.soton.ac.uk/~acr/atsn)

[13] H. Kitano et al., "RoboCup Rescue: search and rescue in large-scale disasters as a domain for autonomous agents research," in *Proc. IEEE Intl. Conf. on Systems, Man and Cybernetics*, pp. 739-743, October 1999.

[14] J. Manyika and H.F. Durrant-Whyte *Data Fusion and Sensor Management: A Decentralised Information-Theoretic Approach*. Ellis Horwood, 1994.

[15] A.O. Hero, K. Kastella, D. Castanon and D. Cochran, Eds. *Foundations of Sensor Management*. Springer, 2007.

[16] F. Zhao and L. Guibas, *Wireless Sensor Networks: An Information Processing Approach*. Morgan Kaufmann, 2004.

[17] N. Xiong and P. Svensson, "Multi-sensor management for information fusion: issues and approaches," *Information Fusion* 3(2): 163-186, 2002.

[18] V. Lesser, C. Ortiz and M. Tambe, Eds. *Distributed Sensor Networks: A Multi-Agent System Perspective*. Kluwer Academic Publishers, 2003.

[19] V.D. Dang, R.K. Dash, A. Rogers and N.R. Jennings, "Overlapping Coalition Formation for Efficient Data Fusion in Multi-Sensor Networks," in *Proc. Twenty-First National Conference on Artificial Intelligence (AAAI-06)*, Boston, USA, 2006.

[20] A. Rogers, R.K. Dash, S. Reece, S. Roberts, and N.R. Jennings, "Computational mechanism design for information fusion within sensor networks," in *Proc. International Conference on Information Fusion (Fusion '06)*, Florence, Italy, 2006.

[21] S. Grime and H. Durrant-Whyte, "Data fusion in decentralised sensor networks," *Control Engineering Practice*, 2(5), pp.849-863, 1994.

[22] S.J. Julier and J.K. Uhlmann, "General decentralised data fusion with Covariance Intersection," in *Handbook of Multisensor Data Fusion*, Eds. D.L. Hall and J. Llinas, SciTech Publishing Inc., 2001.

[23] D.P. Bertsekas and Tsitsiklis, *Parallel and Distributed Computation: Numerical Methods*. Prentice Hall, 1989.

[24] G.M. Mathews, H.F. Durrant-Whyte and M. Prokopenko, "Scalable decentralised decision-making and optimisation in heterogenous teams," in *IEEE International Conference on Multisensor Fusion and Integration for Intelligent Systems (MFI '06)*, 2006.

[25] M. Cetin, L. Chen, J. Fisher, A. Ihler, R. Moses, M. Wainwright and A. Willsky, "Distributed sensor networks: a graphical models perspective," *IEEE Signal Processing Magazine*, July, 2006.

[26] A. Kleiner and M. Göbelbecker, "Rescue3D: Making rescue simulation attractive to the public," Institut für Informatik, Universität Freiburg technical report 00229, 2004.

Acknowledgment

The funding sources and research partner institutions referenced in Section 1.1 are acknowledged. The following colleagues have made significant contributions to the work described here: Peter Bladon, Chris Lloyd and Antony Waldock (BAE Systems); Salah Sukkarieh and David Cole (University of Sydney); Steve Reece (University of Oxford).

David Nicholson
BAE SYSTEMS
Advanced Technology Centre
Sowerby Building, PO Box 5
Filton, Bristol BS34 7QW
United Kingdom
e-mail: David.Nicholson2@baesystems.com

Sarvapali D. Ramchurn and Alex Rogers
Electronics and Computer Science
University of Southampton
Highfield, Southampton, SO17 1BJ
United Kingdom
e-mail: sdr@ecs.soton.ac.uk
        acr@ecs.soton.ac.uk

Whitestein Series in Software Agent Technologies, 33–50
© 2007 Birkhäuser Verlag Basel/Switzerland

Managing Intelligence Resources Using Semantic Matchmaking and Argumentation

Alun Preece, Tomothy J. Norman, Mario Gomez and Nir Oren

Abstract. Effective deployment and utilisation of limited and constrained intelligence, surveillance and reconnaissance (ISR) resources is seen as a key issue in modern network-centric joint-forces operations. In this chapter, we examine the application of semantic matchmaking and argumentation technologies to the management of ISR resources in the context of coalition operations. We show how ontologies and reasoning can be used to assign sensors and sources to meet the needs of missions, and we show how argumentation can support the process of gathering and reasoning about uncertain evidence obtained from various sources.

1. Introduction

Effective deployment and utilisation of limited and constrained intelligence, surveillance and reconnaissance (ISR) resources is seen as a key issue in modern network-centric joint-forces operations. For example, the 2004 report *JP 2-01 Joint and National Intelligence Support to Military Operations* states the problem in the following terms: "ISR resources are typically in high demand and requirements usually exceed platform capabilities and inventory [...]. The foremost challenge of collection management is to maximise the effectiveness of limited collection resources within the time constraints imposed by operational requirements."[1]

Our work focuses upon the application of Virtual Organisation technologies to manage coalition resources. In the past we have shown that an agent-based VOs can manage the deployment and utilisation of network resources in a variety of domains, including e-business, e-science, and e-response [1, 2]. Two distinguishing features of our work are (1)

This research was sponsored by the US Army Research Laboratory and the UK Ministry of Defence and was accomplished under Agreement Number W911NF-06-3-0001. The views and conclusions contained in this document are those of the author(s) and should not be interpreted as representing the official policies, either expressed or implied, of the US Army Research Laboratory, the US Government, the UK Ministry of Defence or the UK Government. The US and UK Governments are authorised to reproduce and distribute reprints for Government purposes notwithstanding any copyright notation hereon.

[1]http://www.dtic.mil/doctrine/jel/new_pubs/jp2_01print.pdf, pages III–10–11, accessed April 27, 2007.

the use of semantically-rich representations of user requirements and resource capabilities, to support matchmaking using ontologies and reasoning, and (2) the use of argumentation to support negotiation over scarce resources, decisions about which resources to use, and the combining of evidence from information-providing resources (e.g., sensors).

In this chapter, we examine the application of (1) and (2) to the management of ISR resources in the context of coalition operations. The first part of the chapter describes an ontology-based approach to the problem of assigning sensors and sources to meet the needs of missions. The second part then looks at how argumentation and subjective logic can facilitate the process of gathering uncertain evidence through actions collectively referred to as sensor probes, and combining that evidence into a set of arguments in support of, and in opposition to, a particular decision.

Our applications involve agents that must cooperate, but still try to maximise their individual utilities, possibly to the detriment of other agents in the system. This type of scenario often appears in military settings, including within coalition operations. Each member of the coalition requires certain assets — including physical assets such as materiel (personnel, vehicles, equipment, etc.), and information assets including various forms of intelligence — to achieve their mission, but these assets are oversubscribed. By advancing arguments as to why they should have the assets, the coalition members may make their own missions more easy to achieve. However, they might have to gather additional information so as to be able to justify their arguments, thus introducing some form of utility cost.

2. Semantic Matchmaking of Sensors and Missions

The assignment of ISR assets to multiple competing missions can be seen as a process comprising two main steps: (1) assessing the fitness for purpose of alternative ISR means to accomplish a mission, and (2) allocating available assets to the missions. Our work draws upon current military doctrine, specifically the Missions and Means Framework (MMF) [3] which provides a model for explicitly specifying a *mission* and quantitatively evaluating the utility of alternative warfighting solutions: the *means*.

Fig. 1 shows how missions map to ISR means. Starting from the top left the diagram sketches the analysis of a mission as a top-down process that breaks a mission into a collection of operations (e.g., search-and-rescue), each of which is broken down further into a collection of distinct tasks having specific capability requirements (e.g., wide-area surveillance). On the right hand side, the diagram depicts the analysis of capabilities as a bottom-up process that builds up from elementary components (e.g., electro-optical/infrared (EO/IR) camera) into systems (e.g., camera turret), and from systems up into platforms equipped with or carrying those systems (e.g., an unmanned aerial vehicle (UAV)).

The way MMF describes the linking between missions and means naturally fits the notion of matchmaking. Matchmaking is basically the process of discovering, based on a given request (e.g., ISR requirements), promising partners/resources (e.g., sensors) for some kind of purpose (e.g., accomplishing a mission). Important issues arise when the

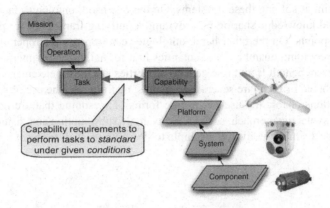

FIGURE 1. Overview of the Mission and Means Framework (MMF)

search is not limited to identity matches but, as in real life, when the objective is finding partners/resources suitable at least to some extent, or (when a single partner cannot fulfil the request) to find a pool of cooperating partners (a sensor network, or a platform equipped with several sensors) able to accomplish it. As this process may lead to various possible matches, the notion of ranking becomes central: to provide a list of potential partners ordered according to some criteria. Due to the diversity of frameworks of application, several communities have studied matchmaking through perspectives and techniques. Recently, semantic matchmaking, which is based on the use of ontologies [4] to specify components, has become a central topic of research in many communities, including multi-agent Systems, Web services and Grid computing.

In particular, we propose the use of ontologies to support the following activities:

- specifying the requirements of a mission;
- specifying the capabilities provided by ISR assets (sensors, platforms and other sources of intelligence, such as human beings);
- comparing — be a process of automated reasoning —the specification of a mission against the specification of available assets to either decide whether there is a solution (a single asset or combination of assets) that satisfies the requirements of a mission, or alternatively providing a ranking of solutions according to their relative degree of utility to the mission.

2.1. Ontologies for matchmaking

People, organisations and software systems need to communicate and share information, but due to different needs and background contexts, there can be widely varying viewpoints and assumptions regarding what essentially the subject matter is. The lack of shared understanding leads to poor communication between people and their organisations, severely limits systems interoperability and reduces the potential for reuse and sharing.

Ontologies[2] aim at solving these problems. On the one hand, ontologies facilitate communication and knowledge sharing by providing a unifying framework for parties with different viewpoints. On the other hand, ontologies can improve interoperation and cooperation by providing unambiguous semantics in a formal, machine-interpretable way. Matchmaking can benefit from these general properties as far as the elements of the process are distributed or there are several viewpoints; additionally, the use of semantically rich specifications enable the use of specific forms of reasoning that are not available when using a syntactic approach, such as for example subsumption and disjunction. Below we provide a simple motivating example to illustrate on such forms of reasoning for matchmaking.

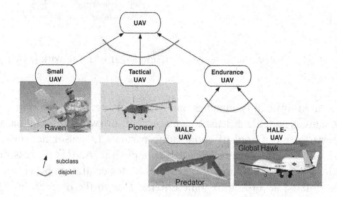

FIGURE 2. Partial classification of unmanned aerial vehicles (UAVs)

Fig. 2 depicts a partial classification of unmanned aerial vehicles (UAVs). The figure shows six classes of UAV, and the various specialisation (subclass) relationships among them. At the top of the classification, the UAV class encompasses all kinds of UAV, which may range in cost from a few thousand dollars to tens of millions of dollars, and range in capability from Micro Air Vehicles (MAV) weighing less than one pound to aircrafts weighing over 40,000 pounds. In this example we include just three categories that are specialisations of the UAV class; these are, from left to right: the Small UAV (SUAV), designed to perform "over-the-hill" and "around-the-corner" reconnaissance; the Tactical UAV (TUAV), which focuses on the close battle in direct response to a brigade commander; and the Endurance UAV (EUAV), which supports a division in deep battle. Further, we have included two categories that specialise the Endurance UAV class: the Medium Altitude Long Endurance (MALE) UAV, designed to operate at altitudes between 5000 and 25000 feet, and the High Altitude Long Endurance (HALE) UAV, designed to function as Low Earth Orbit satellites. The arcs between subclass relationships indicate a disjoint relationship among subclasses; a disjoint relation among a set of classes entails that an

---

[2]For a modern definition of the term, we refer the reader to [5]: "an ontology is a set of logical axioms designed to account for the intended meaning of a vocabulary".

individual cannot belong to more than one of those classes; for example, a UAV that is classified as a Small UAV, cannot be classified as being a Tactical UAV. Next, we introduce some basic examples illustrating specific forms of reasoning enabled by the use of ontologies. Let us suppose that we have the following UAVs available for a mission:

- A Pioneer, which is a TUAV
- A Predator, which is a MALE-UAV
- A Global Hawk, which is a HALE-UAV

Now suppose that as part of a given mission a persistent-surveillance task over a wide area is required to detect any suspicious movement. This kind of task is best served by an Endurance UAV, since it is able to fly for long periods of time. From just the concept definitions we know that: (1) the Pioneer is not an endurance UAV (because of the disjoint relationship among Endurance-UAV and TUAV), and (2) both the Predator and the Global Hawk are Endurance-UAVs (because of the subclass relationships) [3]. Therefore, the matchmaking process will select both the Predator and the Global Hawk as the assets satisfying the specified mission requirements.

Now, suppose that according to the weather forecast, storms are very likely to occur in the area of operations during the surveillance period. Then, the best option would be to use a HALE-UAV, which has the capability of flying "above the weather". Consequently, the matchmaking process would select the Global Hawk as the only asset satisfying the mission requirements.

The UAV examples introduced above refer to a simple form of matching relationships known as *subsumption*, but it is possible to devise more complex information containment relationships and even an ordinal ranking scale comprising several degrees of matching just by using the subclass relationship. Fig. 3 represents graphically the main kinds of matching relations that are found in the literature in terms of information containment, using concepts from the ISR domain. Q denotes a query which specifies some requirements to be met, which in our context are ISR requirements, and $S1 - S5$ denote the specification of components to be matched against Q, which in our domain are associated with ISR assets such as UAVs.

Commencing at the left, our query Q specifies two basic requirements to be met: (1) provide infrared (IR) vision and (2) be able to carry out night reconnaissance. Going from left to right and top to bottom, the figure shows the specification for several assets that verify different types of relation in terms of information containment. Below follows a description of these matching relations listed in decreasing strength order:

1. *ExactMatch(S1, Q)* holds when the specification of a component provides exactly the same type of information described by the query. In the example, $S1$ describes an asset that provides IR vision and is designed to perform night reconnaissance tasks, just as stated in Q. This is represented as $S1 = Q$.
2. *Plugin(S2, Q)* holds when the class of information described by the query subsumes (i.e., is more general than) the class of information specified by the component. In

---

[3]Note that we only state minimum explicit information about the UAVs (e.g., Pioneer is-a Tactical-UAV); everything else is inferred from the concept definitions (e.g., the Pioneer is not a HALE-UAV).

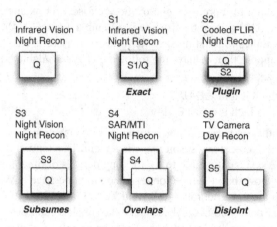

FIGURE 3. Basic matching relationships

the example, the asset described by $S2$ refers to a Cooled FLIR (forward looking IR), which is a specific type of IR camera. This is represented as $Q \subseteq S2$.

3. *Subsumes (S3, Q)* holds when the class of information described by the query is subsumed by the specification of the component, i.e., when the specification of the component is more general than the query. In the example, $S3$ refers to an asset providing night vision capability, which is a more general concept than infrared vision, and also provides night reconnaissance. This is represented as $S3 \supseteq Q$.

4. *Overlaps(S4, Q)*: holds when the query and the specification share some information, but neither one subsumes the other entirely. In our example, $S4$ describes an asset that provides night reconnaissance as required by Q, but the first requirement is not satisfied, since it carries a radar (SAR, Synthetic Aperture Radar) instead of an IR camera, and these two concepts are disjoint. This is represented as $S4 \cap Q$.

5. *Disjoint(S4, Q)*: holds when there is no degree of information containment between the specification of the component and the query. In the example, $S5$ describes an asset that provides TV video and is suited to perform day reconnaissance tasks; radar imagery is disjoint with IR vision, day reconnaissance is disjoint with night reconnaissance, so there is no intersection or information containment between the concepts. This is represented as $S4 \perp Q$.

The kind of matching relationships introduced above are typically used to discover software components or services satisfying some specific requirements. Herein we are proposing to use these kinds of matching relations to discover ISR assets that satisfy intelligence requirements. Although different matchmaking problems could seem very similar in terms of basic matching relationships used, they could differ when considering the matching relationship at the component level, rather than at the attribute level.

2.2. Matchmaking abstract architecture

A matchmaking application is not entirely characterised by the semantic relationships that might be established among concepts. An important issue of a matchmaking application is the distinction between the attribute-level and the component-level: a component may be described by different attributes, and so different matching schemas could be applied to each attribute depending on the particular meaning or role it plays within the component.

In our application, we have identified two main kinds of components to be matched against the ISR requirements of a mission, each one characterised by different attributes that deserve a separate treatment. Note that the kind of capability requirements that are relevant to select a specific kind of sensor are quite different from the requirements that are relevant to select a platform. For example, in order to assess the utility of different sensors it is very important to consider the kind of intelligence to be produced (e.g., Imagery Intelligence (IMINT), Measurement and Signature Intelligence (MASINT), Signals Intelligence (SIGINT), since each type of sensor provides information that supports a different kind of intelligence (e.g., infrared cameras support IMINT, while acoustic sensors support MASINT). Besides, to select a specific UAV for a reconnaissance mission there are other factors to consider, such as the range to the targets of interest, the presence or absence of enemy anti-air assets, and so on. In addition, UAVs are limited in the weight and type of sensors they can carry, and the performance of some sensors may be influenced by conditions that depend on the platform they are attached to, such as the altitude. Therefore, one cannot select UAVs and sensors independently; instead, the interaction between these components must also be taken into account.

To address the issues above, we define an abstract architecture based on three types of components and three kinds of matching relations, as showed in Fig. 4. In each case we build on existing work in defining ontologies for the specific components:

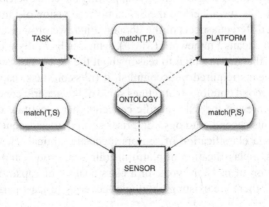

FIGURE 4. Abstract matching architecture

- *Tasks* are the actions to be performed in order to accomplish a mission. A task may have attached environmental conditions (weather, terrain, enemy, etc.) that are expected to impact the performance of a task. We seek to use standardised catalogues of Tasks and Conditions such as those found in the Universal Joint Task List[4].
- *Sensors* are the assets that collect the information required to satisfy the intelligence requirements of a mission. However, sensors do not operate as independent entities, they have to be attached to (or carried by) devices that provide them with energy, protection, mobility, etc. Several ontologies of sensors already exist, e.g., [6, 7].
- *Platforms* are the systems to which sensors are attached so as to get energy, protection, mobility, communication, etc. Platforms include both static and mobile systems operating on land, in sea and air. Again, some work has already been done to create ontologies of these, e.g., [8].

The three components involved and the dependencies between them result in three different matching relations, as follows:

- *Task-Sensor matching*: a sensor S matches a task T, $match(T, S)$, if S provides the information collecting capabilities required to satisfy the intelligence requirements of T.
- *Task-Platform matching*: a platform P matches a task T, $match(T, P)$, if P provides the kind of ISR-supporting capabilities (mobility, survivability, communication) required to perform T.
- *Platform-Sensor matching*: a sensor S matches a platform P, $match(P, S)$, if S can be carried by and is compatible with the characteristics of P.

In order to satisfy the ISR requirements of a mission one needs to select both a platform and a combination of sensors such that the three matching relations of the architecture are satisfied simultaneously.

2.3. Towards a multidimensional solution

Although one can envisage a single ontology supporting the entire sensor-mission matchmaking process, actually we adhere to the Semantic Web vision of multiple interlinking ontologies covering different aspects of the domain. First, we provide an ontology based on the Missions and Means Framework (MMF), which is basically a collection of concepts and properties that are essential to reason about the process of analysing a mission and attaching the means required to accomplish it (mission, task, capability, or asset). Then we provide a second ontology that refines some of the generic concepts in the MMF ontology so as to represent the ISR-specific concepts that constitute our particular application domain. This second ontology comprises several areas frequently organised as taxonomies, such as a classification of sensors (acoustic, optical, chemical, radar) and information sources, a classification of platforms (air, sea, ground and underwater platforms), a classification of mission types, or a classification of capabilities. As noted in the previous section, there are existing ontologies covering at least part of each of these domains.

---

[4]See http://www.dtic.mil/doctrine/jel/cjcsd/cjcsm/m350004c.pdf and http://www.daml.org/2002/08/untl/

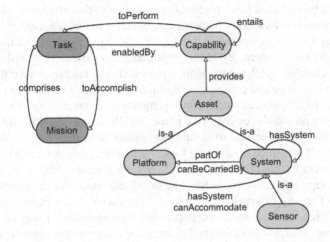

FIGURE 5. Main ontological concepts and their relationships

Fig. 5 shows a high level view of the main concepts and relationships that support our semantic matchmaking approach. On the left hand side, we find the concepts related to the mission: a mission comprises several tasks that need to be accomplished. On the right hand side we find the concepts related to the means: a sensor is a system that can be carried by or constitutes part of a platform; inversely, a platform can accommodate or have one or more systems, and both platforms and systems are assets; an asset provides one or more capabilities; a capability can entail a number of more elementary capabilities, and is required to perform certain types of tasks and inversely, a task is enabled by a number of capabilities.

In the next section, we focus on the use of argumentation to manage the gathering of evidence from a set of sensors and sources assigned to a task.

3. Arguing About Evidence in Partially Observable Domains

In this section, we examine how argument may be used to reason about sensor assignment based on evidential and diagnostic reasoning. Informally, we are trying to address situations where different agents, each with their own goals and viewpoints, are attempting to reach a shared agreement about the state of a subset of their environment. By reaching agreement, they may take decisions about how their actions should be coordinated. We further assume that the environment is partially observable, and that any information about it is obtained through the use of (possibly incorrect) evidence. Finally, we assume that the agents are self interested. The argumentation approach has a number of advantages over competing methods, including understandability, improved running time and ease of knowledge representation.

Without a trusted third party, a centralised solution to this problem is difficult. Our proposed approach involves the agents engaging in dialogue with each other, exchanging arguments, and obtaining evidence (possibly via existing sensors) for additional information about the environment. By basing arguments on evidence, a shared world view can be constructed. To tackle the problem, a representation mechanism for the environment, agents' knowledge and arguments is required, as well as a method for determining which conclusions are justified when opposing arguments interact. A specification is also needed, detailing how dialogue may take place. Finally, agents must be able to decide which arguments to advance, and what sensors to probe for evidence.

Prakken [10] identified these as the logical, dialectic, procedural and heuristic layers of an argument framework. Our logical layer is built around Subjective Logic [11], allowing us to represent concepts such as likelihood and uncertainty in a concise and elegant manner. The way in which arguments are constructed in our framework and used at the dialectic level is intended to support a rich representation of arguments; we are able to represent concepts such as accrual of arguments, argument schemes and argument reinforcement in a natural manner. While the logical and dialectic layers are domain independent, acting as a general argument framework, the explicit introduction of evidence at the procedural level allows us to attack our problem.

Evidence is gathered via sensors, where a sensor refers to anything that can determine the state of a portion of the environment. Multiple sensors may exist for certain parts of the environment, and some of these sensors may be more accurate than others. Finally, sensors may not perform their services for free. Thus, sensors capture an abstract notion of a source of evidence within our framework.

At the procedural level, agents engaging in dialogue, taking turns to advance arguments and probe sensors in an attempt to achieve their goals. In this context, an agent's goal involves showing that a certain environment state holds. We assume that an agent associates a utility with various goal states. Our heuristic layer guides an agent and tells it what arguments to advance, and which sensors to probe during its turn in the dialogue game.

The logic of our framework is built on Subjective Logic [11], which, in turn, is based on Dempster-Schafer theory. We may assign an *opinion* to predicates representing portions of the environment. These opinions are $\langle belief, disbelief, uncertainty \rangle$ triples [5].

Jøsang defined a large number of operators that are used to combine opinions, some of which are familiar such as conjunction and disjunction, and some less so such as abduction. We look at three operators, namely negation, discounting, and consensus.

The propositional negation operator calculates the opinion that a proposition does not hold. A negated opinion's belief is equal to the original opinion's disbelief, while the original disbelief becomes the opinion's belief. Uncertainty remains constant.

Discounting is used to model hearsay. That is, given that an agent has an opinion a about agent β's reliability, and that β has an opinion x about something, without any additional information, α will have an opinion $a \otimes x$, where $\otimes$ is the discounting operator.

---

[5]This is in fact a simplification, Subjective Logic ordinarily uses 4-tuples, with the forth element representing atomicity.

The independent consensus operator gives the opinion an imaginary agent would have about x if it had to assign equal weighting to different opinions x_1, x_2 about a state of the world x. It is represented as $x_1 \oplus x_2$.

3.1. The Framework

Following Prakken's model [10], we build our framework in layers, starting at the logical layer, where we describe how an argument is constructed. In the dialectic layer, we look at how arguments interact, and then show how agents may engage in dialogue in the procedural layer. Finally, in the heuristic layer, we show how agents can decide which lines of argument should be advanced in a dialogue.

Facts in our model are represented as grounded predicates, and have an associated opinion. An argument is an instantiated argument scheme [12] linking facts to other facts. Argument schemes are common, stereotypical patterns of reasoning, often taking on a non-deductive or non-monotonic form. A simple argument scheme (Modus Ponens) could be represented as follows:

$$(ModusPonens, \{holds(A), implies(A, B)\}, \{holds(B))\}, F, true)$$

Here, F is:

$$\omega(holds(B)) = \begin{cases} \langle 0, 0, 1 \rangle & b(holds(A)) < 0.5 \text{ or} \\ & b(implies(A, B)) < 0.5 \\ \omega(holds(A)) & b(holds(A) < b(implies(A, B)) \\ \omega(implies(A, B)) & \text{otherwise} \end{cases}$$

where $holds(A)$ and $implies(A, B)$ are the premises of the argument scheme (i.e., these facts must hold for the argument scheme to be instantiated into an argument). $holds(B)$ is the conclusion of the argument scheme (i.e., this fact may be instantiated if the argument scheme is applicable), F is a function allowing us to compute the opinion for the conclusion based on the opinions associated with the premises, and finally $true$ is an *applicability* function, stating any restrictions on the application of the argument scheme. We make use of first order unification to transform an argument scheme into a concrete argument. any symbols in capital letters are unified with facts, as done in prolog, so as to instantiate the scheme.

Until now, we have described what individual arguments look like. However, arguments do not exist in isolation. Instead, they interact with each other, reinforcing or weakening opinions about predicates in the process. Unlike most other argumentation frameworks, we do not explicitly model rebutting and undercutting attacks to show how arguments interact. Instead, we use the concept of accrual of arguments to allow for both argument strengthening and weakening. To represent interactions between arguments, we must be able to answer the following question: what happens when two different arguments have opinions about a (partially shared) set of predicates in their conclusions?

The independent consensus operator gives us a default technique for applying accrual. Thus, given a set of arguments for and against a certain conclusion, and given no extra information, we apply the consensus operator based on the opinions garnered from the arguments to arrive at a final opinion for the conclusion.

While some researchers have suggested that accrual of arguments is an argument scheme and can be treated as such (arguably, for example [13]), Prakken's view, in our understanding, is that the best way to handle accrual of arguments is by following a two stage process. First, determine what arguments may enter into an accrual, and second compute the effects of the accrual. We agree that accrual of arguments cannot be treated as "just another" argument scheme due to its role and nature. We believe, however, that in certain situations (usually obeying principle 1), accrual of evidence can be treated as an argument scheme. The way in which our framework aligns these two views is one of its most unique aspects.

Informally, given multiple arguments for a conclusion, we apply the standard consensus rule. However, if an argument is advanced which subsumes (some of the) arguments which take part in the consensus, the subsumed argument's conclusions are ignored, and the subsuming rule is used instead. If any of those arguments are attacked and defeated, then our accrual rule is itself defeated, allowing all its undefeated (and previously subsumed) members to act again. If some of the newly activated sub-members were, in turn, part of accruals, those accruals would enter into force again.

Given these underpinnings, it is possible to provide an algorithm for evaluating how sets of instantiated arguments interact. Such an algorithm operates in a way similar to the way reasoning occurs in probabilistic networks, and is best explained by thinking of our sets of arguments and predicates as a graph. Both predicates and arguments can be thought of as nodes, with a directed edge between the two if the predicate appears in the premises or conclusions of an argument. The edge enters the argument in the case of the predicate being a premise, and exits the argument otherwise.

To operate, our algorithm requires an argument graph, as well as a starting set of opinions. We assume that these opinions are not under dispute, and the associated nodes must, therefore, have no edges leading into them. Our algorithm then propagates these opinions forward through the graph, until all applicable arguments in the graph have been taken into account. The specific details of the algorithm appear in [14].

At this point, we have a way of determining which conclusions hold given a set of arguments. It is now possible to define a procedure for how the set of arguments is generated. This can be done in two phases. In the first, a dialogue between agents may be defined. This states when an agent may make an utterance, and what form these utterances should take. We assume that agents take turns to speak, and that the game ends when both agents pass (i.e., say nothing) during their turn.

Since we are interested in arguing about evidence in partially observable domains, we assume that the environment holds a number of sensors. These sensors may be probed to obtain opinions about the value of various relations. In practise, sensors may be agents, static parts of the environment, or some other entity capable of providing an opinion about the environment. We assume that multiple sensors can give opinions about the same relations, and that some sensors are more reliable than others.

During their turn, an agent may advance a connected set of arguments, and probe a number of sensors. These sensor probings are one way to associate an opinion with a fact. The other way is to have the fact be the conclusion of an argument.

At each step in the dialogue, an opinion is calculated for every fact. When participating in the game, an agent must decide which utterance to make. We associate a cost to
probing actions, and a utility gain to the showing that certain facts hold in the world. Then
the agent selects the utterance that maximises their utility. In effect, the agents perform
one step lookahead during their turn. Increasing the level of lookahead requires some form
of opponent modelling.

3.2. An example scenario

In this section, we describe a dialogue in a hypothetical sensor assignment scenario. A
commander, fronted by an agent α, has a mission (labelled $mission(m)$) to accomplish.
To successfully execute the mission, he requires the use of a sensor package that can be
deployed on either a Predator UAV, or a Sentry UGV (with deployment on the UAV preferred by the commander). Another agent β, is also present in the system. Both agents
share some knowledge, but both also have private beliefs. β could represent another commander, a member of a coalition, or, though not explicitly examined in this scenario,
someone with their own goals, some of which may not be compatible with α's mission.
We assume that certain sensors have already been deployed in the field, and that the agents
have access to these and other sources of information such as GIS systems. α must argue
with β in an attempt to allocate resources for its mission. In the interests of clarity, the
description of the dialogue that follows is semi-formal.

Assume the agents have the following argument schemes available to them:

Name	Premises	Conclusions
ModPon	$A, B, implies(A, B, C)$	C
HumInt	$atLocation(E, L), claims(E, A),$ $inArea(A, L)$	A
MisAss	$capable(T, R), available(R),$ $hasTask(M, T)$	$assigned(M, R)$
M_1	$higherPriority(M, N), uses(N, R)$	$reassignReq(N, M, R)$
M_2	$reassignReq(N, M, R),$ $reassign(M, R)$	$assigned(M, R)$
D_1	$ugv(U), taskLocated(T, L),$ $hasRoad(L)$	$capable(U)$
D_2	$ugv(U), taskLocated(T, L), mud(L)$	$capable(U)$
D_3	$ugv(U), taskLocated(T, L), mud(L),$ $hasRoad(L)$	$capable(U)$

We do not show the admissibility and mapping functions in this table, but assume
that they are unique to their associated argument scheme.

Some arguments here are very general, for example, $ModPon$ represents standard
two premise Modus Ponens. Others, such as $HumInt$ and $MisAss$, are specific to the
military domain. The former, similar to Walton's argument from expert opinion [12], represents an argument based on information from "expert" human intelligence. The latter
argument scheme allows agents to reason about when a resource may be assigned to a
task. M_1 and M_2 are very specific to the military domain, and represent how agents may
reason about task assignments, while the remaining argument schemes are used to reason

about the applicability of a UGV to different types of domains. Note that D_3 is able to handle more specific cases than D_1 and D_2.

α would like to assign either a UGV or a UAV to his mission (preferring a UAV), and thus has the goals

$$assigned(mission(m), uav(predator)), assigned(mission(m), ugv(sentry))$$

With a higher utility being given to the former goal.

Both agents are aware of the following facts:

$hasTask(mission(m), task(t))$ $higherPriority(mission(m), mission(n))$
$capable(t, uav(predator))$ $implies(recentRain(l), sand(l), mud(l))$
$ugv(sentry)$ $taskLocated(t, l)$
$atLocation(h, l)$

Agent α also believes that $available(uav(predator)), hasRoad(l)$ and, believes there is a good chance that, if necessary $reassign(mission(m), uav(predator))$ would work. It also believes that no rain has fallen at $l,$ and that the human intelligence assets would agree with it, i.e., $claim(h, \neg recentRain(l))$ and $inArea(l, \neg recentRain(l))$.

Agents can probe a GIS system to determine the status of $hasRoad(l)$ at very little utility cost, while $recentRain(l)$ and $sand(l)$ would cost α more utility. Probing whether the UAV is available can be done at very little cost by looking at different inventory databases. We also define two expensive sensors for the reassignment request and the reassignment itself. These represent the cost of going up the chain of command to ask for the UAV/UGV to be reassigned. Finally, it is possible to probe the opinion of the human intelligence for details such as the $claim()$ predicate, but this is very expensive as the location of the assets might be compromised.

Agent α begins the conversation by making the utterance

$$((MisAss, \{hasTask(mission(m), task(t)), capable(t, uav(predator)),$$
$$available(uav(predator))\}, \{assigned(mission(m), uav(predator))\}),$$
$$\{available(uav(predator))\})$$

In other words, it attempts to check that the predator UAV is available for the mission, and assign it (if possible). We assume that the probe succeeds.

β responds with its own sensor probe $(, \{available(uav(predator))\})$, as it believes the UAV is not available.

When this returns an opinion of $\langle 0.1, 0.9, 0 \rangle$, α's argument is nullified. α now has two options. It may either ask to get the UAV reassigned to it (which would involve a large cost in utility), or may attempt to use the UGV. Since low cost sensor probes are available to it, it will get a greater utility gain by attempting to use the UGV than by following the former route. It thus makes the utterance:

$$(\{(D_1, \{hasRoad(l), taskLocated(t, l), ugv(sentry)\}, \{capable(t, ugv(sentry)\}),$$
$$(MisAss, \{hasTask(mission(m), task(t)), capable(t, ugv(sentry)),$$
$$available(ugv(sentry)))\}, \{assigned(mission(m), ugv(sentry))\})\},$$
$$\{available(ugv(sentry)), hasRoad(l)\})$$

In other words, it claims that since there are roads at the location, and since the UGV is available, it can use it for its mission.

β believes that (due to rain and sand), mud exists at the location. This leads to the utterance:

$$((\{ModPon, \{recentRain(l), sand(l), implies(recentRain(l), sand(l), mud(l))\},$$
$$\{mud(l)\}), (D_3, \{ugv(sentry), taskLocated(t, l), mud(l), hasRoad(l)\},$$
$$\{capable(t, ugv(sentry))\}), \{recentRain(l), sand(l)\})$$

Argument D_3 subsumes D_1, meaning that $capable(t, ugv(sentry))$ is no longer believed.

α can now either probe human intelligence to check for the presence of mud, or attempt to get the mission's resources reassigned (we assume that the UAV was assigned to $mission(n)$). The latter option yields it more utility, and it makes an utterance using argument schemes M_1 and M_2, while probing $reassign$ and $reassignReq$.

β has no more responses, and thus passes, as does α, meaning that the UAV will be assigned to the mission.

Obviously, the dialogue described here is simplified. In a realistic scenario, the agents would have access to more information and many more argument schemes. Fig. 6 illustrates the argument graph that resulted from this dialogue, though for clarity, part of the graph is omitted.

While α has managed to get the UAV assigned, it paid a steep utility cost. α would have preferred to get the UGV assigned to it without having to have asked for the reassignment of resources, but would then not have been able to complete its mission (due to β's criticism).

Once the dialogue terminates, predicates are associated with opinions. Depending on the form of the admissibility function, they, or their negation may be judged to be admissible. Thus, for example, if $assigned(mission(m), uav(predator))$ exceeds a certain threshold, it is assumed to be assigned to mission m.

3.3. Discussion

Our framework was designed to allow for complex argument to take place, particularly in the domain of evidential reasoning. Uncertainty is a key feature of such domains, hence our decision to base our framework on Subjective Logic. Catering for uncertainty in argumentation frameworks is by no means new. Pollock [13] made probability a central feature of his OSCAR architecture. We disagree with his extensive use of the "weakest link" principle, however, believing that, while it may hold in general, it is not always applicable (as mentioned in [15]). His use of probability, rather than uncertainty is another point at which our approaches diverge.

Our use of Subjective Logic as the basis of the framework provides us with a large amount of representational richness. Not only are we able to represent probability (via belief), but we are also able to speak about ignorance (via uncertainty). Differentiating between these two concepts lets us represent defaults in a natural, and elegant way. A default can be represented by specifying, within the A function, that a conclusion may hold as long as the disbelief for a premise remains below a certain threshold. By requiring

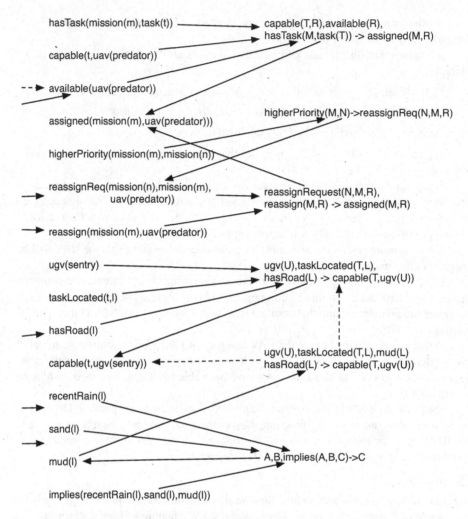

FIGURE 6. The argument graph for the dialogue. The second use of the *MisAss* argument scheme is omitted. Solid arrows indicate support for an argument or predicate, while dashed lines represent an attack or weakening. Arrows with no source indicate sensor probes.

that belief remain above some threshold, normal premises can also be represented. A simple example of this was provided in the previous section, where everyone, by default, is assumed to be an expert. Burden of proof [16] is very closely related to defaults, and we model it in the same way.

Argument schemes have been extensively discussed in the literature (see for example [17, 12]). A small, but growing number of argumentation frameworks provide explicit support for argument schemes (e.g., [18]). We believe that supporting argument schemes in our framework not only enhances argument understanding, but that such support also provides clear practical advantages, including the separation of domain and argument knowledge, re-usability, and a possible reduction in computational complexity when deciding what arguments to advance. The separation between arguments and agent knowledge created by argument schemes raises the intriguing possibility of the modification and dynamic creation of argument schemes during a dialogue.

The interplay between sensors and arguments is an area in which little formal work has been done [19]. While our model is very simple, it elegantly captures the fact that sensor data is inherently unreliable in many situations. Enriching our model of sensors is one area in which we plan to do future work.

4. Conclusions

In this chapter, we have described how two aspects of our work on managing resources in Virtual Organisations can be applied to the problem of deploying and utilising intelligence assets in coalition operations. We have shown how modern military doctrine, in the form of the Missions and Means Framework, can be captured in a semantically formal representation, allowing sensors and other ISR resources to be assigned to a mission through matchmaking reasoning. This approach has the advantages that the MMF concepts are familiar and transparent to users (e.g., commanders) and the assignments are logically sound.

We have also shown how argumentation can be used to manage the process of gathering and reasoning about evidence from sensors and sources. Because such sources are fallible, and the military domain typically involves environments that are only partially observable, we needed to devise a novel framework for argumentation in domains containing uncertainty. The concept of argument schemes is built into the framework, allowing for a rich set of primitives to be utilised in the argumentation process. We have also attempted to cater for other important concepts in argument such as accrual of arguments, defaults, and burden of proof. While the lowest levels of the framework are general enough to be applied to almost any area in which argument is used, the higher levels are aimed at evidential reasoning, incorporating abstract models of sensors and the notion of obtaining information from the environment.

References

[1] T. J. Norman, A. D. Preece, S. Chalmers, N. R. Jennings, M. M. Luck, V. Dang, T. Nguyen, V. Deora, J. Shao, W. A. Gray, N. J. Fiddian, "CONOISE: Agent-based formation of virtual organisations," *Knowledge-Based Systems* 17(2–4), 2004, pp. 103–111.

[2] A. Preece, S. Chalmers, C. McKenzie, "A reusable commitment management service using semantic web technology," *Knowledge-Based Systems* 20(2), 2007, pp. 143–151.

[3] J. H. Sheehan, P. H. Deitz, B. E. Bray, B. A. Harris, A. B. H. Wong, "The military missions and means framework," in *Proc. of the Interservice/Industry Training and Simulation and Education Conference*, 2003, pp. 655–663.

[4] T. R. Gruber, "Toward principles for the design of ontologies used for knowledge sharing," *Journal of Human Computer Studies* **43(5/6)**, 1994, pp. 907–928.

[5] N. Guarino, "Formal ontologies and information systems," in *Proc. of the 1st International Conference on Formal Ontologies in Information Systems (FOIS-98)*, IOS Press, 1998, pp. 3–15.

[6] D. McMullen, T. Reichherzer, "The common instrument middleware architecture (CIMA): Instrument ontology & applications," in *Proc. of the 2nd Workshop on Formal Ontologies Meets Industry*, Trento, Italy, 2006, pp. 655–663.

[7] D. Russomanno, C. Kothari, O. Thomas, "Building a sensor ontology: A practical approach leveraging ISO and OGC models," in *Proc. of the 2005 International Conference on Artificial Intelligence*, CSREA Press, 2005, pp. 637–643.

[8] L. Bermudez, J. Graybeal, R. Arko, "A marine platforms ontology: Experiences and lessons," in *Proc. of the 2006 Workshop on Semantic Sensor Networks*, Athens GA, USA, 2006.

[9] C. A. Reed, T. J. Norman, eds., *Argumentation Machines: New frontiers in argumentation and computation*. Kluwer, 2003.

[10] H. Prakken, G. Sartor, "Computational Logic: Logic Programming and Beyond," in *Essays In Honour of Robert A. Kowalski*, Part II. Volume 2048 of LNCS, Springer-Verlag, 2002, pp. 342–380.

[11] A. Jøsang, "A logic for uncertain probabilities," *Int. Journal of Uncertainty, Fuzziness and Knowledge-Based Systems* **9**, 2001, pp. 279–311.

[12] N. D. Walton, *Argumentation Schemes for Presumptive Reasoning*. Erlbaum, 1996.

[13] J. L. Pollock, *Cognitive Carpentry*. Bradford/MIT Press, 1995.

[14] N. Oren, T. J. Norman, A. Preece, "Subjective logic and arguing with evidence," *Artificial Intelligence Journal*, 2007, to appear.

[15] H. Prakken, "A study of accrual of arguments, with applications to evidential reasoning," in *Proc. of the 10th Int. Conf. on Artificial Intelligence and Law*, 2005, pp. 85–94.

[16] D. N. Walton, "Burden of proof," *Argumentation* **2**, 1988, pp. 233–254.

[17] F. Bex, H. Prakken, C. Reed, D. Walton, "Towards a formal account of reasoning about evidence: Argumentation schemes and generalisations," *Artificial Intelligence and Law* **11**(2-3), 2003, pp. 125–165.

[18] B. Verheij, "Dialectical argumentation with argumentation schemes: An approach to legal logic," *Artificial intelligence and Law* **11**, 2003, pp. 167–195.

[19] N. Oren, T. J. Norman, A. Preece, "Argumentation based contract monitoring in uncertain domains," in *Proc. of the 20th Int. Joint Conf. on Artificial Intelligence*, Hyderabad, India, 2007, pp. 1434–1439.

Alun Preece, Tomothy J. Norman, Mario Gomez and Nir Oren
Department of Computing Science, University of Aberdeen, Aberdeen, AB24 3UE, UK
e-mail: apreece@csd.abdn.ac.uk
         tnorman@csd.abdn.ac.uk
         mgomez@csd.abdn.ac.uk
         noren@csd.abdn.ac.uk

Whitestein Series in Software Agent Technologies, 51–72
© 2007 Birkhäuser Verlag Basel/Switzerland

Agent Applications in Defense Logistics

Todd Carrico and Mark Greaves

Abstract. During World War II, US Military logistics was the envy of the world. By Desert Storm / Desert Shield, overwhelming mass had become the supply strategy of the day. In the years following Desert Storm, the military set out to reinvent its logistics strategy through Focused Logistics and the Defense Advanced Research Projects Agency (DARPA) was charged with developing the next generation information technology to make it a reality. This chapter reviews the vision, concepts and technologies of DARPAs Advanced Logistics Project (ALP) and UltraLog Project as well as the development, experimentation, demonstration, transition and eventual commercialization of the Cognitive Agent Architecture (Cougaar).

1. The Vision of Future Military Logistics

The end of the Cold War era has resulted in significant changes to our national military strategy. We have significantly decreased the size of our armed forces, our forward-deployed capability, and our supply inventories. As a result, our capability to rapidly deploy and sustain a fighting force anywhere in the world has become more critical than ever before.

Joint Vision 2020 sets the stage for the US military's organization and missions of the future. Joint Vision 2020 identifies "**Focused Logistics**" as one of the key components for achieving full spectrum dominance in future conflicts. Focused Logistics, as defined by Joint Vision 2020, is " ... *the ability to provide the joint force the right personnel, equipment, and supplies in the right place, at the right time, and in the right quantity, across the full range of military operations. This will be made possible through a real-time, web-based information system providing total asset visibility as part of a common relevant operational picture, effectively linking the operator and logistician across Services and support agencies*" [1].

The **Advanced Logistics Project (ALP)** was a joint DARPA/Defense Logistics Agency (DLA) research project, which was investigating, developing, and demonstrating technologies that will make a fundamental improvement in logistics planning and execution efficiencies, ultimately affording total control of the logistics pipeline. It was defining, developing, and demonstrating advanced technologies that enable forces and sustainment material to be deployed, tracked, sustained, refurbished, and redeployed more efficiently and effectively than ever before, during peacetime and contingency operations.

The ALP program has directly addressed the shortcomings of the existing logistics support systems and has developed automated, multi-echelon, real-time collaborative technologies for the joint logistics communities. These technologies providing logisticians and warfighters with unprecedented capability to plan, execute, monitor, rapidly replan and re-execute logistics support, even while assets are enroute to the theater of operations. Thus the goal of ALP is to meet the objectives of Focused Logistics through advanced information technology.

The revolutionary core technology developed under the ALP effort is an advanced cognitive-based agent architecture, called **Cougaar (Cognitive Agent Architecture)**. The objective of the DARPA follow-on program **UltraLog** is to build upon the progress and successes of the Cougaar agent architecture developed under ALP, while extending that architecture in the areas of security, robustness and scalability.

The intent of UltraLog is to develop a highly survivable agent infrastructure that is able, at a minimum, to support all aspects of **Focused Logistics**. The scope of operations for UltraLog is therefore the scope of operations for Focused Logistics. Since the completion of UltraLog, the Cougaar / ALP / UltraLog technologies have found several applications in the DoD, one of which, the Adaptive Logistics project, is outlined briefly. All of these efforts demonstrate the power and effectiveness of agent technology to address the many diverse challenges of the Defense Logistics problem domain.

2. The DARPA Advanced Logistics Project (ALP)

Focused Logistics, as described in Joint Vision 2020 [1], describes well the challenges of Military Logistics in the 20th Century.

"Focused logistics will effectively link all logistics functions and units through advanced information systems that integrate real-time total asset visibility with a common relevant operational picture" [1].

"[...] logisticians will achieve real-time, total asset visibility from the depot or warehouse to the user. That will eliminate the need to move and stockpile huge quantities of supplies "just in case" they're needed" [2].

"Developments in Automatic Identification Technology (AIT) integrated into automated information systems (AIS) [...] will enhance automated tracking of assets throughout the world" [3].

Joint Vision 2020 reached one critical conclusion regarding logistics - the military MUST get control of the logistics pipeline. It must have tighter ties between operations and logistics, acquire material faster, and make smarter use of transportation resources. The only way this can be done is through aggressive development of advanced information technology that will cause a fundamental change in the way logistics planning and operations are conducted today.

The solution in the past has been to substitute mass where we lack agility and velocity, thereby overwhelming the problem with brute force. However, in doing so we incur an enormous expense. During desert shield sealift moved nearly 3.5 million short tons of equipment at a cost of nearly $2B. In analyzing this action, it was realized that a great deal of inefficiency was afforded to the lack of visibility into the logistics process, coordination between operations and logistics, and optimization of the scheduling process. It is estimated that we could have produced the same results in 100 fewer days and with 1M tons less cargo if we could have solved these problems. To meet this stressing requirement, logistics and transportation assets must be used more effectively and efficiently than ever before.

To meet this challenge, the Defense Advanced Research Projects Agency, in conjunction with the Defense Logistics Agency (DLA), the United States Transportation Command (USTRANSCOM), and in coordination with the Joint Staff Directorate of Logistics (JS/J-4), undertook an initiative called "The Advanced Logistics Project" or ALP. This project was seeking a quantum improvements

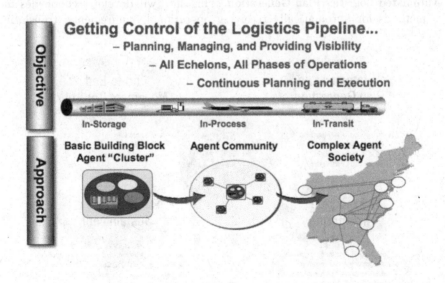

FIGURE 1. The ALP Approach to Control of the Log Pipeline.

in military logistics and realize the Joint Vision 2020 goal of Focused Logistics. Achieving Focused Logistics requires a dynamic multi-functional logistics information environment capable of sharing real-time information with users at every level of command, in every service, dispersed across the entire globe. ALP's vision was transform the current stove-piped, disparate, and compartmentalized logistics environment into one that is highly automated and fully integrated to ensure concurrent operational and logistics planning. ALP developed and demonstrated new enabling technologies to achieve unprecedented control over the logistics pipeline.

Control of the logistics pipeline, as shown in Fig. 1, demands a radical shift in the way planning and execution is done today. Operations and logistics must be viewed as a tightly coupled closed loop system. Operators and logisticians, at all levels, must be brought together in a distributed interactive planning environment to plan, execute, monitor, and rapidly replan. The future concept of operations is envisioned as an interoperable environment for the operators in J3 and logisticians in J4 to coordinate their activities. To achieve this vision, DARPA set out to develop technology that speeds logistics planning, execution monitoring and replanning; ensures accurate, reliable, and timely information; and creates plan "monitors" that allow the accuracy of the information system and provide early warnings of events that deviate from the plan.

2.1. ALP Grand Challenges

ALP identified four Grand Challenges, shown in Fig. 2, that provided direction and set the capability objectives for the program.

Automated Logistics Plan Generation. This effort will develop technologies and methods for automatically receiving operational requirements; translating

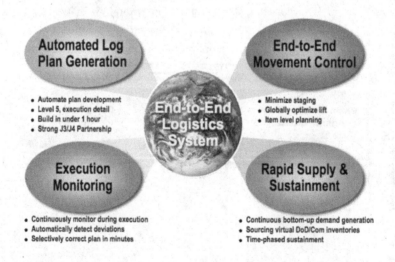

FIGURE 2. The ALP 4 Grand Challenges.

them into logistics support requirements; generating below the line force lists and sustainment needs; identifying critical items; automating the requisition process; identifying and scheduling organic and commercial lift assets; estimating risks and other cost trade-offs; developing logistics courses of action; and/or automated generation of TPFDD-like logistics support plans.

End-to-End Movement Control. This effort will develop technologies and methods to maintain end-to-end control of the transportation/logistics pipeline through the automated development of responsive transportation plans and continuous monitoring techniques.

Execution Monitoring. This effort will develop technologies and methods for providing users at all echelons with the ability to assess the logistics situation by converting logistics data into information rich visualizations that can be used to understand the current situation and project future states.

Rapid Supply. This effort will develop technologies and methods necessary to establish interoperable connectivity and access to DOD and commercial vendors, suppliers and manufacturers to increase material readiness, decrease cycle times for satisfying materiel requirements while reducing DOD inventory and overhead costs.

2.2. Building Operations-Logistics Plans

The over-arching vision of the Advanced Logistics Project is an end-to-end prototype logistics system that enables operations, planning, and logistics personnel to work together to develop multiple courses of action with their corresponding detailed logistics plans using real world data. With this extremely detailed plan, we can enter into execution, quickly and with confidence that our plans are logistically supportable. We can use technologies such as plan sentinels to watch critical components of the plan during execution, and when deviations are detected, localized replanning will be automatically triggered. This forms a continuous cycle, as shown in Fig. 3, between execution monitoring and continuous replanning - where the system is always executing and replanning those components affected by detected deviations. The global living logistics plan is a key concept of the ALP vision. It is a plan that contains all the information in great detail. It is a globally distributed plan, fed continuously by real world data. From this detail, we can form a common picture of logistics, which when tied to operations, provides a total operational picture.

2.3. Demonstrating Command and Control in the Logistics Domain

In the functional demonstration provided in May '01, ALP presented a Cougaar-based end-to-end global logistics prototype for planning and performing execution monitoring of a small-scale contingency in East Africa. This plan represented the deployment of over 33,000 people, 20,000 MEI's, all 4 services and included key elements of DLA, TRANSCOM, supply classes 1,3,4,5,8, & 9, detailed transportation planning, ISB, 3-levels of medical care and much more, as summarized in Fig. 4.

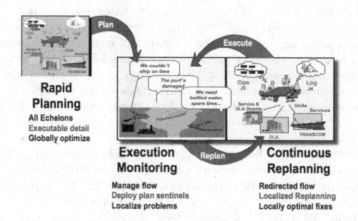

Rapid
Planning

All Echelons
Executable detail
Globally optimize

Execution
Monitoring

Manage flow
Deploy plan sentinels
Localize problems

Continuous
Replanning

Redirected flow
Localized Replanning
Locally optimal fixes

FIGURE 3. The Planning, Execution, Dynamic Replanning Cycle.

In that demonstration, we showed different slices of a very complex distributed logistics plan that was developed in under an hour by the collaborative effort of hundreds of Cougaar agents. The demonstrated slices (views of the logistics plan in execution) included the collaborative processes of demand generation, sourcing, inventory management, and distribution. We showed details of this distributed logistics plan in terms of temporal, geographic and organizational structures. Also, during the demo one got a sense of the ability to monitor during execution and dynamically re-plan in the face of external changes or modified

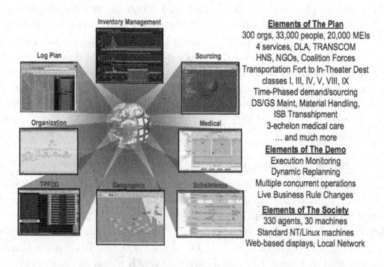

FIGURE 4. Demonstrated ALP Functions and Technology.

operational requirements. Observers saw the support for multiple concurrent operations with the detailed planning for both of those operations under the natural contention that occurs when limited resources must be shared between multiple operations. In addition, we demonstrated how you could identify and in some cases actually make real-time changes to the business rules that drive the underlying behavior of the agents and their role in the larger global logistics plan. This was an example of a 300 organization society, represented by over 300 agents. They were executed on 30 standard mid-range machines in a LAN configuration, but could just as easily have been distributed geographically all over the world with some additional network latency. The functional demo also gave a sense of how the operational and logistics interactions would occur, starting with the operational requirements, moving through the demand generation, sourcing, inventory management and transportation planning, then into the execution monitoring and dynamic re-planning. All of the processes collaborative support the creation of this very large distributed logistics plan. Users can then interact with those plans and processes to understand the results of that planning process and through execution monitoring how well operations are achieving those plans.

Over the five years of the program, the Advanced Logistics Project demonstrated the technology to achieve the vision of an end-to-end logistics system. ALP, in partnership with DLA and TRANSCOM, developed and matured the world's largest distributed cognitive agent architecture that is now available as open source. ALP has demonstrated an end-to-end prototype logistics system that is capable of developing a level 5 logistics plan in under an hour. It is capable of monitoring the execution of that plan against multiple simultaneous operations and can demonstrate the collaboration of hundreds of organizations working together to manage the details of global logistics. ALP has developed a powerful cost-effective technology approach to realizing focused logistics and ultimately revolutionizing our global logistics business process.

By the end of the ALP project, as shown on the scorecard in Fig. 5, it had demonstrated accomplishment of the 4 grand challenges, the underlying technology objectives that are required to achieve our larger vision for which the program was created. These include the technology challenge of creating this large scale distributed agent system, fine grain distribute information management, virtual global operations and logistics plan and representing the human cognitive model in our software for the capture of human planning and business processes. In addition the defined objectives, during the course of this program a number of other significant accomplishments were achieved. The first and foremost is that the program created the worlds most advanced agent architecture, the Cognitive Agent Architecture (Cougaar), which is detailed in Section 6. The program applied the Cougaar technology to logistics to create a prototype system that has built the fastest ever construction of a level 5 logistics plan. Where it takes humans weeks to build that level fidelity in a logistics plan our prototype can do it in about an hour. As a result, we ALP delivered a mature distributed information system infrastructure that can support the next generation of global logistics enterprise.

Objective	Evidence	Assessment
ALP Grand Challenges:		
• Fast, Level 5 Logistics Plan Generation	Demo	G
• End-to-end Movement Control	Demo/Analysis	G
• Rapid supply and sustainment	Demo/DLA	G
• Execution Monitoring/Dynamic Replanning	Demo/Exp	G
ALP Technology Challenges		
• Large-scale distributed agent systems	Proto/Exp	G
• Fine-grained information management	Proto	G
• Virtual global operations/logistics plan	Proto	G
• Human Cognitive Model in Software	Demo/Exp	G
Feasibility: Total control of the Logistics Pipeline	Proto/Analysis	G
Scalability: Global Logistics Business Process	Exp/Analysis	G

FIGURE 5. Report Card on the ALP 4 Grand Challenges.

Ultimately we have unleashed this power of agent technology for global operations and defense logistics.

3. The DARPA UltraLog Project

The UltraLog project built on the success of the Advanced Logistics Project and the sophistication of the Cougaar Agent Architecture to tackle one of the most difficult problems in computer science: the creation of a robust, reliable distributed system, with assured performance bounds, operating over an unreliable network and in extreme conditions of fault and failure. ALP created the basic technologies needed to achieve the challenging computational goals of Focused Logistics in JV2010 and JV2020. In order to be deployable, however, the Cougaar technologies developed by ALP had to be further refined and made survivable for the most hostile and chaotic battlefield environments. The central hypothesis of UltraLog was that survivability in distributed systems can be assured by leveraging the inherent agility and semantic interaction models of software agent systems, and developing agent-specific algorithms to guarantee the robustness, scalability, and security of the core data and information processing. As shown in Fig. 6, UltraLog aimed to create a resilient distributed system that can protect and adapt itself under harsh, dynamic conditions.

Following in the steps of the ALP project, the UltraLog project defined its own Grand Challenge. The Grand Challenge of the UltraLog project started with a logistically more complex version of ALP's Challenge: to create a society of over 1000 medium complexity agents, whose job was to jointly create and maintain a

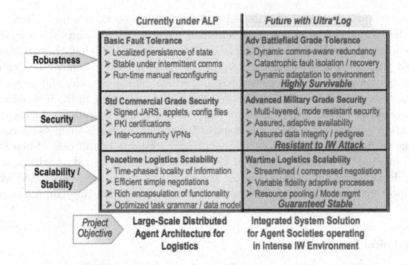

	Currently under ALP	Future with Ultra*Log
Robustness	**Basic Fault Tolerance** ➤ Localized persistence of state ➤ Stable under intermittent comms ➤ Run-time manual reconfiguring	**Adv Battlefield Grade Tolerance** ➤ Dynamic comms-aware redundancy ➤ Catastrophic fault isolation / recovery ➤ Dynamic adaptation to environment *Highly Survivable*
Security	**Std Commercial Grade Security** ➤ Signed JARS, applets, config files ➤ PKI certifications ➤ Inter-community VPNs	**Advanced Military Grade Security** ➤ Multi-layered, mode resistant security ➤ Assured, adaptive availability ➤ Assured data integrity / pedigree *Resistant to IW Attack*
Scalability / Stability	**Peacetime Logistics Scalability** ➤ Time-phased locality of information ➤ Efficient simple negotiations ➤ Rich encapsulation of functionality ➤ Optimized task grammar / data model	**Wartime Logistics Scalability** ➤ Streamlined / compressed negotiation ➤ Variable fidelity adaptive processes ➤ Resource pooling / Mode mgmt *Guaranteed Stable*
Project Objective	**Large-Scale Distributed Agent Architecture for Logistics**	**Integrated System Solution for Agent Societies operating in Intense IW Environment**

FIGURE 6. Enhancing Cougaar with Advanced Survivability.

TPFDD over a period representing 180 days of sustained military operations in a major regional contingency. UltraLog employed a highly realistic military operations scenario of ALP scale, involving an initial 180 day plan with deployment, RSOI, PREPO, and operations, and included 6 major (and multiple minor) OPlan changes, 28,000 MEIs, 33,000 personnel, and featuring supply class I, III, V, and IX planned to level 5 detail. However, UltraLog specified that this Challenge would be achieved in one of the most challenging computational contexts imaginable: with the global agent system operating under continuous directed adversary information warfare attack, and suffering both targeted and random infrastructure losses ranging up to 45% of the total CPU, memory, and network bandwidth capability. In this context, the UltraLog system had to exhibit not more than 20% capabilities degradation and not more than 30% performance degradation in its performance on the logistics planning tasks. By the final year of the project, UltraLog was to demonstrate successful completion of this Grand Challenge.

3.1. UltraLog Approach

UltraLog takes a different technical approach to system survivability than traditional information assurance techniques. Most survivability technologies in existence today view the individual computer and network as the critical components requiring maximum protection. Typical security products are designed to thwart attacks by detecting and combating them before they can cause damage. In contrast, while UltraLog does assume that our logistics information systems will incorporate current best practices in information assurance, UltraLog also assumes that these best practices will occasionally fail under determined attack. In a heterogeneous, dynamic, distributed system of systems, no defense is invulnerable. Therefore, a logistics infrastructure will never be secure and robust against all possible attacks. Because of this, UltraLog presupposes that the aggressors can and will be able to occasionally penetrate the network, damage or destroy computing resources, acquire passwords, introduce malicious code, and stress the logistics system in various malicious ways. Instead of protecting individual pieces of hardware or networks, UltraLog technologies are designed to protect vital logistics information wherever it resides and ensure that critical logistics business processes continue to be successfully executed even under extreme conditions. When conditions preclude normal operation of the logistics system, UltraLog will manage system degradation such that the most critical functions continue unabated while less important information processing is deferred until operating conditions improve.

3.2. Technical Focus

The technical focus of UltraLog is to seek out and develop a suite of software technologies that can make distributed software agent applications sufficiently secure, robust, and scalable to meet the demands of the most difficult wartime environments. Operationally, the most important military impacts of distributed agent systems derive from their ability to integrate data not just globally, but also across the three major levels of military engagement: strategic, operational, and tactical. The UltraLog vision is to produce the first example of a system that successfully and survivably bridges the gap between the predictable, non-chaotic world of high-level strategic logistics planning and the much more chaotic, time-critical and failure-prone world of operational and tactical logistics. The distributed agent architecture of UltraLog makes this bridging feasible through a seamless and robust distributed system framework. This framework is augmented by the on-the-spot ability of agents both to collect and fuse data locally, and to rapidly re-assign resources on a task-priority basis from whatever pool of networked resources is currently available, even if that pool has been damaged or reduced in size. The intelligent employment of these and other capabilities makes it possible to fuse, deliver and safeguard the exact, real-time data that high-level planners need to make effective, time-critical decisions, while providing field-level operational personnel with the precise information needed to move forward with confidence.

3.3. UltraLog Extensions to Cougaar

As noted previously, the UltraLog Project developed technologies that **exploit the unique characteristics of software agents** to create survivable distributed planning systems. In the areas of **scalability technologies** the program developed and integrated technologies for variable fidelity processing, load balancing, dynamic reconfiguration and problem splitting, and distributed control. In addition, UltraLog pursued technologies to scale to high-fidelity force structures, more complex logistics demands, and agent counts greater than 1000 agents while not sacrificing

	2000	2001	2002	2003	2004	Stress	Technology Approach
Scalability	R	Y	Y	G	G	Wartime loads (complexity)	Variable fidelity processing, opportunistic planning
	R	R	Y	Y	G	Wartime loads (variability)	Predictive load balancing (threatcon, P(fail))
	R	R	Y	G	G	Wartime loads (stress overlaps)	Defense deconfliction (Adaptivity engine and POMDPs)
	R	R	Y	Y	Y	Interaction instabilities	Dampers; fast time queueing prediction
	R	Y	Y	Y	G	Scaling of nodes and agents	Distributed adaptivity engine, communities, policies
	R	R	Y	Y	G	Scaling logistics problem	Service discovery, agent reaffiliation
Security	Y	G	G	G	G	Fraudulent, untrusted code	Secure Java class loader, signed class files
	R	G	G	G	G	Untrusted communications	Prohibition policies, PKI infrastructure
	R	Y	G	G	G	Insecure / dangerous code	Java Security Manager, M&R subsystem, policies
	R	R	Y	G	G	Corruption of persisted state	Encryption, certificate infrastructure
	R	R	R	Y	G	Unauthorized processing	Access control binders, policies, community/agent RBAC
	Y	Y	Y	G	G	Erroneous component behavior	Tech spec binder protection
	Y	G	G	G	G	Component masquerade	Certificate-based authentication
	R	Y	Y	G	G	Compromised agents	Component restoration, identity and certificate leasing
	R	Y	Y	G	G	Servlet-based attacks	Attribute certificates, checkpoint restoration
	R	R	R	Y	Y	Intrusion	Cert revocation, community-based scope limits, M&R
	R	R	Y	Y	G	Compromised communities	Policy-based behavior declarations; secure NTP
	R	R	Y	Y	G	Snooping	Traffic masking, trust models, user authentication
	Y	G	G	G	G	Message intercept	Encryption, authentication, PKI
Robustness	R	Y	G	G	G	Processing failure (occur)	Liveliness checking, persistence
	R	Y	Y	Y	G	Processing failure (restore)	Checkpoint rehydration, intelligent resynch
	R	R	Y	Y	G	Network failure	Predictors; communities; QoS-based messaging
	R	Y	G	G	G	Network disconnect	Multiple message transports
	R	Y	Y	G	G	Processing contention	Task-based prioritization
	R	Y	Y	G	G	DOS attack	Predictors, multiple communication mechanisms

FIGURE 7. Technologies, Stresses and Status for UltraLog Survivability.

performance or overloading network resources. In the areas of **robustness technologies**, the basic Cougaar architecture was extended to leverage loose coupling and semantic agent communication to build agent systems with global fault tolerance and recovery, complex workflow dynamism, predictors, and service diversity. On the security side, UL incorporated **security technologies** that enabled construction of a distributed trust agent security model by developing techniques for agent based data protection, role based access control, policy distribution and enforcement, and security monitoring and response. The extensive suite of technologies and techniques integrated into the core Cougaar framework are shown in Fig. 7. The results were an extremely survivable and adaptive infrastructure that could continue to operate even under extreme kinetic and information warfare stresses.

3.4. Key Experimental Findings

The UltraLog program had a stronger element of experimentation and analytic evaluation than the ALP project before it. As a result, significant experimental system, functional and survivability analysis was performed against the increasing complex experimental baseline developed for the program. This section briefly presents some of those results.

3.4.1. System Findings. The capabilities and performance to build a complex logistics plan continued to grow throughout the ALP and UltraLog programs. By the end of the UltraLog program, the ability to reliably create a high quality logistics plan, even under significant infrastructure losses, was proven. We had improved performance and configuration adaptation to the point that significant infrastructure loss, in excess of 40%, resulted in a negligible impact on completion time and a controllable degradation in product quality. These results are shown in Fig. 8 - each dot in the graph represents a distinct experimental run over the entire simulated 180 day campaign, with different combinations of infrastructure loss.

3.4.2. Functional Findings. UltraLog's functional analysis focused on the effectiveness of the agents to operate as a system, performing the functions of logistics, under the various forms of stress. The effectiveness of the system dealt with many aspects of the functional processes to include quality, timeliness, and accuracy. Under independent assessment by groups of active and retired military logisticians, UltraLog system demonstrated the ability to build and maintain realistic high fidelity logistics plans under stress, and dynamically replan as required to cope with changes in the requirements, environment or availability of resources. As the system got larger and more complex, additional management components were required to monitor the system and resources and take the measures necessary to ensure proper, secure, sustained operations. Fig. 9 shows the growth in the number of functional and management agents over the course of the program.

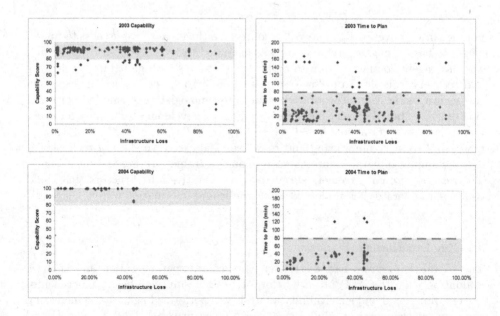

FIGURE 8. UltraLog System Planning Performance under Stress.

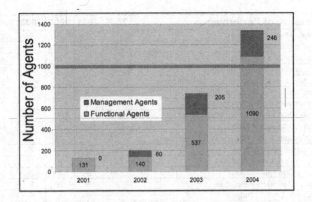

FIGURE 9. Functional and Management Agents in the Experimental Baseline.

3.4.3. Survivability Findings. Because evaluation was a key aspect of the UltraLog program, the program employed several independent Red Teams. In the annual evaluation, the development team would stand up the experimental testbed and the Red Team would employ various techniques to attempt to compromise the operation of the system. Prior to the evaluation, the read team was given full access to the source code, configuration, topology, and other aspects of the system operation. The attacks and stresses were applied in categories, with the results of the system performance being assigned a value from 1 to 10, where 1 was poorest and 10 was best performance against the attack. A value of 0 was assigned where no survivability measures existed and no evaluations were performed. Fig. 10 shows the survivability findings of the evaluations for the UltraLog testbed over the course of the program. By the end of the program, few of the stresses had more than a mild impact on the operation of the system and no attacks were regularly and completely successful in bringing the operation of the testbed below the defined minimal operational level.

4. The Adaptive Logistics Project

In 2006, the Logistics Innovation Agency (LIA) developed a recommended Army Sense and Respond Logistics (S&RL) Vision and demonstrated the capability of S&RL by incorporating intelligent agent technology and integrating disparate data sources to more efficiently and effectively manage logistics information.

Intelligent agent technology represents a core component of the Adaptive Logistics Capability Tool (ALCT) and builds on ALP and UltraLog core technologies as transitioned to LIA. The technical advancements of the ALCT are in the development and maintenance of a real time shared situational picture based on the Situational Reasoning Framework extensions to Cougaar developed as part of the ActiveEdge commercialization.

Measure of Performance	2000	2001	2002	2003	2004
Obtain Platform Access	1	2	5	8	8
Invalid User Access	0	0	8	9	9
Unauthorized User Action	0	0	8	9	9
Circumvent Platform Security	0	0	0	9	9
Modify Codebase for One or More Nodes	0	0	0	8	8
Load Malicious Plugin or Agent	1	3	4	8	8
Circumvent Policy Enforcement	N/A	1	7	7	7
Application Level Denial of Service	0	0	7	7	7
Manipulate Agent Mobility	N/A	N/A	3	6	8
Manipulate Agent Society Relationships	0	0	3	4	8
Corrupt Blackboard	0	0	7	7	8
Circumvent Cryptography	1	7	8	8	8
Hijack Communications	1	8	9	9	9
Spoof Malicious Messages	0	8	8	8	8
Network Traffic Analysis	0	5	5	5	5
Information Leaks	2	5	8	8	8
Exploit Network Infrastructure	0	0	2	4	4
Disable Critical Node (Single point of failure)	0	0	5	8	8
Modify System Policies	0	1	7	7	7
Hinder Attribution of Agent/User Actions	N/A	N/A	8	9	9

FIGURE 10. UltraLog Survivability Findings.

Adaptive Logistics requires: (1) a network-centric environment that connects logisticians with operations and intelligence to interpret the commander's intent in terms of missions, environment, desired outcomes, and priorities; (2) the capability to create adaptive Communities of Interest (COIs) that are responsible for planning for, executing, and monitoring logistics responses; (3) analytics that generate alternative courses of action, their feasibility in terms of resource requirements and availability, and the consequent risks for each alternative; and (4) cognitive decision support tools that weigh the factors driving decisions within the cycles of decision makers from the point-of-effect through the strategic base. These requirements were largely satisfied by the Cougaar architecture, but lacked support of the shared situation representation and reasoning.

4.1. Situational Understanding as the Basis of Optimized Planning

The objective of the ALCT project was to provide key aspects of the Sense and Respond Logistics (S&RL) vision in a manner that, for a set of meaningful questions, **creates situational understanding and actionable information where none previously existed**. The ALCT dynamically constructs a sourcing and distribution plan for in theater resourcing of material requests. It builds and maintains a theater wide situational picture of supply, transportation and routing, as shown in Fig. 11, and uses that understanding to find feasible solution sets. From that set, the system chooses the best solution given the current policies and establishes that as sourcing and distribution plan for that requisition, coordinating the solution with all the units involved. As shown in Fig. 11, Unit demand requisitions (1) flow up to the (2) Theater Support Command (TSC). Requisitions are then

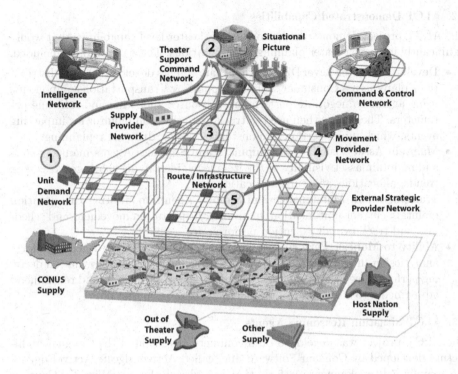

FIGURE 11. The ALCT Theater Agent Planning Network.

analyzed through an optimization algorithm for the "best value" supplier (SSA) (3) and the transportation unit (4) within theater. Once the transportation and SSA is known we find (5) the optimal route based on time and cost and other user defined business rules and weightings. Any requisitions not serviced in-theater will be put back into the normal process and sourced from CONUS. By tying every component of the plan into the situation, events that impact a required resource of that plan - road segment, delivery truck, etc - can immediately be linked back to the affected plans for notification and dynamic replanning. The situational picture is a virtual construct composed of a series of community networks: units, supply, transportation, routing, etc. Each network is composed of the units performing those functions, using the power of distributed intelligent agent technology to realize local decision support and local situational representations for each unit in theater. At organizations like the TSC, elements of the individual situational pictures and networks are combined to form the aggregate state of the theater and performance of ongoing operations.

4.2. ALCT Demonstrated Capabilities

The ALCT project demonstrated a core set of theater level capabilities that would significantly improve theater planning and operations. These capabilities included:

- **Develop a Theater Level Distribution Plan:** Agents develop real time distributions plans across Consumer, Supply Support, & Transportation components, using agents to negotiate performance, resource allocation and schedule parameters. The plan is then used to track execution and monitor for impacting events, which under certain circumstances trigger dynamic replanning.
- **Maintain Asset Visibility of Equipment and Supplies:** Agents manage assets and maintain asset visibility at the item level, identifying shortages, excesses, trends, allocations and current location.
- **Transportation, Maintenance and Supply:** Agents monitoring the situation maintain current unit location, monitor transportation movement and schedules and track overall execution performance.
- **Ability to Monitor Performance by Theater Level Metrics:** Agents perform analytics on the historical, current and projected situation information deriving performance metrics which are used to flag problem areas and recommend adjustments to the operational policies to improve performance.

4.3. ALCT Situation Reasoning Agents

The ALCT project was developed on a commercial version of the Cougaar architecture developed by Cougaar Software, Inc. called ActiveEdge®. ActiveEdge [8] is a commercial development platform that provides all the capabilities of Cougaar described in Section 6, as well as a variety of additional capabilities like a workflow engine, rule engine, device interface layer, advanced visualization environment, integrated Semantics support [7], SOA and JMS support as well as a Situational Reasoning Framework (SRF) subsystem for deep situational reasoning and Distributed Data Environment (DDE) subsystem for advanced dynamic mediation. The key technical advancement demonstrated by the ALCT effort was the ability to build and maintain a large scale, complex situational picture composed of individual local situational pictures maintained at the unit level. The higher echelons composed the elements of the lower echelon situational pictures to create the composites. The actual composition and analysis was done by a special class of agents known as situational reasoning agents which used a variety of correlation, reasoning and pattern filtering to update the situational picture as new information flowed in. ALCT demonstrated that this approach, tuned to the data sets and functional reasoning appropriate for in-theater logistics, was effective against theater scale data sets with reasonable performance.

5. The Cognitive Agent Architecture (Cougaar)

To understand the power of applying the Cougaar technology to solve complex problems, it is helpful to first have a basic understanding of the technology itself.

Cougaar stands for the Cognitive Agent Architecture because its design is based on a model of human cognition. Cougaar marries the complex, yet agile human cognitive process for reasoning, decomposing and solving problems with the speed, accuracy and tireless capacity of modern computers. This model is the heart of the technology, and represents a powerful way of representing distributed collaborative tasking and execution for complex problems. This representation also allows the expression of problems and their solutions in terms familiar to people from their everyday activities, easing the human-system shared-understanding problem. Development of solutions utilizing the cognitive model enable greater efficiency of development, enhanced operational flexibility and reliability, and lower life-cycle costs.

5.1. The Cognitive Model

Humans approach problems using a set of high-level strategies that they apply iteratively and recursively to classify, decompose, reason, plan and then accomplish each task or sub-task. These strategies, often done in collaboration or coordination with other humans, are assembled patterns of cognitive processes which may include:

- Gathering: Get information from the outside world
- Supporting: Receive/recognize tasking or relevant changes
- Decomposing: Break a problem into smaller sub-problems
- Acting: Perform some action that impacts with real entities in real-time
- Delegating: Assign some problem(s) to supporting resources for solution
- Consolidating: Take a number of independent pieces and handle them as a single problem
- Assessing: Continually monitor progress to make sure things are proceeding as planned, and correct/react accordingly
- Reporting: Report back to outside world

The Cougaar infrastructure has a logical representation for each of those cognitive elements and utilizes a dynamic workflow engine to build the patterns, interconnect the representations of the cognitive components and accomplish the task. The workflow may exist across multiple agents, where pieces may be shared representing coordinated activities or referenced representing the delegation of one cognitive element to another party.

In the Cougaar architecture, these cognitive elements are called PlugIns, because they are modular components that are assembled within an agent to give that agent its functional behavior. The core set of Cougaar PlugIn types includes the following:

- Expander (Decomposing): Break down task into a workflow of sub-tasks
- Allocator (Delegating): Allocate tasks to appropriate resources for final handling or further disposition
- Aggregator (Consolidating): Join a set of tasks into a single super-task

- Assessor (Monitoring): Assess the current state against known plans and objectives, and force replanning when necessary
- Data Plugin (Gathering): Read/write new/changed information from/to external data sources
- UI Plugin (Out-of-band reporting): Provide external user interface. (Inter and intra agent reporting supported by agent infrastructure)
- Execution (Acting): Interact with external entities, objects, systems

The Cougaar approach is to decompose a problem and problem solving process, into reasonable, testable building blocks, each oriented to a class of PlugIn. An agent's behavior will be realized from the emergent behavior of the assemblage of PlugIns in its configuration. This concept is shown in Fig. 12.

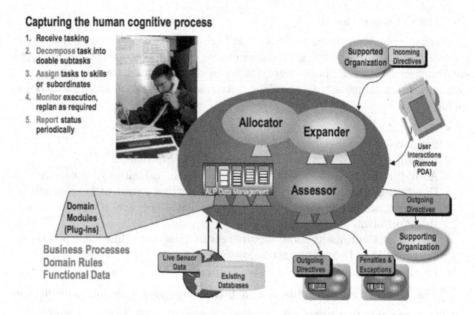

FIGURE 12. The Cougaar Cognitive Model.

5.2. Communication, Tasking and Collaboration

Cougaar represents and communicates with the human functional domain, which is mapped into the base cognitive model through a rich task grammar that forms the lingua franca of a Cougaar system. Tasks and their workflows form a functional process map for the problem domain being addressed by a Cougaar system in a form that is both intuitively understandable to humans and sufficiently precise to support automated reasoning by the intelligent agents. This rich language representation makes the integration of disparate legacy systems simple and straightforward by mapping each system's schema or interface into the domain task grammar through Data PlugIns.

The task grammar base types are made up elements like tasks, assets, expansions, aggregations, and allocations. These elements make up the building blocks of workflows, which are built and maintained on a distributed blackboard. The blackboard of each individual Cougaar agent represents a part of the larger distributed community blackboard, managed in a distributed fashion across the whole Cougaar community. Each agent owns its blackboard and its contents are visible only to that agent. All sharing of blackboard state is done by explicit push-and-pull of data through inter-agent tasking, query, or publish & subscribe services. In this way, a Cougaar agent is able to maintain fine-grained state information locally and only share pieces of the plan with other agents where coordination, service dependencies, or reporting is required. This approach makes the fine-grained management of information scalable and efficient. Cougaar also supports a rich notion of past, present and future time, allowing it to plan over the same assets in different time periods, reason about potential outcomes, and establish specific monitors to look for evidence indicating the result of some task action.

Another fundamental concept of distributed management of the blackboard is that of "managed inconsistency". There is no overarching central control within the Cougaar architecture that synchronizes operations or imposes inter-agent transaction boundaries. Each agent works independently and asynchronously on messages passed from one another, and responds independently and asynchronously on responses received from other agents. No inter-agent prioritization or ordering is imposed. As a result, these features allow the agents to work efficiently and independently with no need to deliberately ensure data or process synchronization or have a precise shared operational clock. However, what this independence does impose is that the distributed blackboard, taken in the aggregate across the community, is never guaranteed to be in a consistent state. The blackboard of any given agent will be consistent as interactions with the blackboard from PlugIns are transaction-bound, but by design there may be brief periods of inconsistency between different agents blackboards. This appears at first glance to be a flaw in the system, but in reality it is one of the many elements that give it so much power. By not demanding continuous consistency, we dramatically reduce the communications, computation and infrastructure requirements on the system. We also enable a clean and natural support for dynamic reconfiguration and operations under intermittent communications.

5.3. Planning and Execution

A Cougaar multi-agent system is continuously operating, monitoring its state and the state of its environment for changes that require a reevaluation of its past, present and future actions and their expected outcomes. When an unexpected change occurs, the plugins within each agent are notified based on their subscriptions and can examine the change to see if some action or replanning is required. If it does take action by adding, removing, or changing tasks or their dispositions, these changes are propagated by the Cougaar infrastructure to the impacted agents. Because these changes are only propagated to affected agents, the impact of a small change will be isolated to a small part of the system and the impact of a large change will propagate as needed, but will not cause unnecessary recomputation. Special mechanisms are built into the system to ensure stability and prevent the system from oscillating or going chaotic.

Cougaar supports the implementation of execution monitoring and dynamic replanning through its assessor and data plugins. Data plugins are responsible for monitoring external state and updating the agent's view of external data as it changes by modifying objects on the agent's blackboard. Assessor plugins are responsible for continually monitoring the state of the blackboard for self-consistency and triggering a re-evaluation of the agent's solutions as appropriate. This separation of responsibilities results in a loose, flexible coupling with external data systems while still allowing full internalization of the external data.

The use of standard Internet technologies like XML, Java, and HTTP make integrating and interfacing Cougaar with other systems much easier than with proprietary technologies. Cougaar is implemented completely in the Java Programming Language, which has become the programming language of choice for Internet applications. It also uses XML and related technologies, which are now embraced by all major organizations as the best way to build systems for maximum interoperability. As these Internet technologies mature and improve, Cougaar systems will be able to take advantage of these improvements immediately.

5.4. Summary of Key Benefits of the Cougaar Approach

The primary benefits of using the Cougaar architecture are the following:

Intelligent Behavior through the Human Cognitive Process. By utilizing a fundamental framework based on the human cognitive process, Cougaar agents can reason, plan, execute, monitor and assess in much the same manner as humans do. Further, the cognitive model serves as a natural way of decomposing a problem or problem domain resulting in better solutions that are more understandable and less prone to developer error. With each element of the cognitive model mapping cleanly to a cognitive process, business processes can quickly and dynamically be assembled and implemented to solve emerging problems, allowing the system to adapt to new situations and conditions.

Scalable Distributed Computing. Agents in general, but Cougaar especially, embody all the best features of distributed computing. Further, Cougaar was specifically designed to be efficiently scalable to extremely large societies. Through hierarchical name service, dynamic discovery, adaptive role-relations and other qualities, Cougaar operates well in unstable, dynamic environments with special safeguards to ensure data integrity and preserve system stability. Using message-based coordination with information sharing through a partitioned blackboard, complex multi-organization problems can be solved using the agent approach that truly realize the collaborative computing concept.

Integrated Planning and Execution. Most systems segregate planning and execution, making dynamic execution induced replanning difficult and inefficient. Cougaar, through the cognitive model, enables these activities to be seamlessly interwoven empowering the continuous planning, execution and dynamic replanning which is Cougaar's trademark. Further, for planning systems which include a simulation and projection capability, Cougaar blurs the line between simulation and execution by utilizing the same business processes in either a real or virtual context. This largely avoids the behavior skew and behavior abstraction problems which cause many simulations to inaccurately reflect the behaviors of the real systems they are modeling.

Evolvability of the Solution. The Cougaar technology and developmental approach allows applications to evolve. By this, we mean applications can be deployed a component at a time, in a heterogeneous environment, thus avoiding the tradition risk and cost involved with complete software overhauls. Changes impacting any discreet unit of functionality can occur without impact to any other part of the system or network. The distributed agent approach provides a way to introduce rapid, low cost, low risk changes, additions and improvements to a suite of applications when changes are available or required. This capability dramatically reduces the overall lifecycle costs and development/maintenance time for the project(s).

Pure Java, hosted on Desktop and Embedded systems. Since Cougaar solutions are developed purely in Java, the agents can run on virtually any computer platform. With the extension to embedded devices through Micro Cougaar, even embedded components can support Cougaar agents. The write-once, run-anywhere capability of Java means solutions are never locked into a hardware platform and can immediately take advantage of new hardware advances.

6. Conclusions

This paper presents the origin, concepts and application of Cognitive Agent Architecture in the domain of military logistics. As Cougaar has been 10 years in the making, it also reflects the evolution of the most significant investment in the application of agent technology to military logistics ever undertaken. The successful development and demonstration of the Cougaar technology, in both the ALP and UltraLog programs, demonstrates the power of agents to deal with massive scale problems in complex environments. It also provides solid evidence to the general value and capabilities of the agent-oriented approach to solving complex distributed planning and execution problems. The adoption of the Cougaar technology, by both military and industry, suggests that the Cougaar technology has a future in a variety of operational systems, such as the Army's FCS program and commercial products, such as Cougaar Software's ActiveEdge®. As of this printing, ActiveEdge (www.cougaarsoftware.com) was the first commercial distributed intelligent agent development platform based on the DARPA-sponsored Cougaar technology.

7. Acknowledgement

Cougaar is the result of a significant, sustained investment by the Defense Advanced Research Projects Agency (DARPA) under the Advanced Logistics Program (ALP) and UltraLog (UL) Project. Through this vision and support, one of the most powerful intelligent distributed agent frameworks in the world was born. The development of the core Cougaar technology would not have been possible if not for the outstanding team researchers, functionals, developers, integrators and managers at BBN, as well as the many supporting teams at Cougaar Software, SAIC, SRI Northrop Grumman, LMI, Sandia National Labs, Lockheed Martin, MITRE, Boeing Phantomworks and many others. DARPA has made the Cougaar technology open source, which is freely available under a modified BSD license at www.cougaar.org. The work on the Sense & Respond Logistics / Adaptive Logistics was sponsored by the Army Logistics Innovation Agency (LIA) and performed by the team of Cougaar Software, Inc., SAIC, Dimensions International and others under several past and ongoing DoD contracts. The views and conclusions contained herein are those of the authors and should not be interpreted as representing the official policies or endorsements, either expressed or implied, of DARPA, LIA, the Army, the Department of Defense or the U.S. Government.

References

[1] Joint Visions 2020, JCS, http://www.dtic.mil/jv2020/jvpub2.htm

[2] Gen. H. H. Shelton, Chairman of the Joint Chiefs of Staff, "Focused Logistics and the way ahead," Jan, 1999, http://www.dla.mil/Dimensions/janfeb99/Shelton.htm

[3] Focused Logistics Roadmap, JCS, August 1997,
    http://www.dtic.mil/jcs/j4/projects/foclog/jlrmap.html

[4] Cognitive Agent Architecture (Cougaar), http://www.cougaar.org

[5] UltraLog security services project site, http://securitycore.cougaar.org/

[6] ActiveEdge Platform, http://www.cougaarsoftware.com/

Todd Carrico
Former DARPA ALP and UltraLog Program Manager
Currently: President / CTO, Cougaar Software, Inc.
e-mail: tcarrico@cougaarsoftware.com

Mark Greaves
Former DARPA UltraLog Program Manager
Currently: Program Manager, Vulcan Inc.
e-mail: markg@vulcan.com

Whitestein Series in Software Agent Technologies, 73–96
© 2007 Birkhäuser Verlag Basel/Switzerland

AGENTFLY:
Towards Multi-Agent Technology
in Free Flight Air Traffic Control

David Šišlák, Michal Pěchouček, Přemysl Volf, Dušan Pavlíček,
Jiří Samek, Vladimír Mařík and Paul Losiewicz

Abstract. Ever rising deployment of *Unmanned Aerial Assets* (UAAs) in complex military and rescue operations require novel and innovative methods for intelligent planning and collision avoidance among a high number of heterogeneous, semi-trusted flying assets in well specified and constrained areas [1]. We have studied the free flight concept as an alternative to the classical, centralized traffic control. In free flight the unmanned aerial assets are provided with flight trajectory that has been elaborated without consideration of other flying objects that may occupy the same air space. The collision threads are detected by each of the aircraft individually and the collisions are avoided by an asset-to-asset negotiation. Multi-agent technology is very well suited as a technological platform for supporting the free-flight concept among the heterogeneous UAAs. In this chapter we present AGENTFLY, multi-agent system for free-flight simulation and flexible collision avoidance.

1. Introduction

AGENTFLY is a software prototype of a multi-agent simulator of unmanned aerial vehicles air traffic control supporting the free flight concept. All aerial assets in AGENTFLY are modeled as asset containers hosting multiple intelligent software agents. Each container is responsible for its own flight operation. The operation of each vehicle is specified by an unlimited number of time-specific, geographical way-points. The operation is tentatively planned before take-off without consideration of possible collisions with other flying objects. During the flight performance, the software agents hosted by the asset containers detect possible collisions and engage in peer-to-peer negotiation aimed at sophisticated re-planning in order to avoid the collisions. The implemented simulator demonstrate readiness of the multi-agent technology for distributed, flexible, and collision-free coordination among heterogeneous, autonomous aerial assets (manned as well as unmanned) with a potential to (i) fly a higher number of aircrafts, (ii) decrease requirements for human operators and (iii) allow a flexible combination of cooperative and non-cooperative collision avoidance.

AGENTFLY is build on top of the $\mathcal{A}$-globe multi-agent platform [12]. $\mathcal{A}$-globe provides flexible middleware supporting seamless interaction among heterogeneous software, hardware and human actors. $\mathcal{A}$-globe outperforms available multi-agent integration toolkits by its ability to model rich environments in which agents interact, by its support of full code migration and by its support for scalable experiments. For more information see Appendix A. Current AGENTFLY implementation provides a distributed model of flight simulation and control, time-constrained way-point flight planning algorithm avoiding specified no-flight zones and terrain obstacles, flexible collision avoidance architecture – cooperative and non-cooperative, connectors to external data sources (Landsat images, airports monitors, no-flight zones, cities), 2D/3D visualization including a web-client access component, and a multi access operator - a component facilitating real-time control of selected assets.

The present work mainly addresses the problem of distributed collision avoidance among autonomous aerial assets using multi-agent technology [11] – each UAA is represented by an agent container hosting different functional agents [15]. Each UAA is controlled by a single, dedicated agent. The presented collision avoidance architecture provides capability to integrate several different collision avoidance algorithms that plan the runtime trajectory of each individual UAA. Such architecture supports operation of the group of cooperative UAA within the environment hosting other non-cooperative flying objects (e.g., civilian air traffic or manned aircrafts in the same area).

Cooperative collision avoidance, the deconfliction process between two or more interacting and cooperating aerial assets, is based on using different collision metrics [6] and negotiation protocols. Recently, the centralized solution has been replaced by various distributed approaches facilitating deployment of e.g., principled negotiation [16], Monotonic Concession Protocol (MCP) [19, 9] for collision avoidance in between of two assets [17] or extensions towards groups of multiple UAAs [13]. Such approach can be slightly altered to optimize social welfare instead of individual goals in the group of UAAs. There are also various approaches based on the game theory (e.g., [5]) available in the research community.

Optimization of non-cooperative collision avoidance algorithms (deconfliction process of an individual aircraft facing a non-cooperative, possibly hostile object) [14, 3] allows optimal solving of the collision with a non-cooperative flying object (obstacle). These algorithms perform well when coping with a single alien flying object, but they cannot be extended to a situation with several flying objects, located nearby. Moreover they cannot be used simultaneously with other cooperative algorithms applied for the cooperative collisions at the same place. The research work reported in this contribution was motivated by designing such a non-cooperative collision avoidance method that does not suffer from these weaknesses.

In this chapter we briefly present the architecture of the AGENTFLY system. The chief technical contribution of the presented work is, however, in the collection of agent-based collision avoidance methods and the flexible multi-layer deconfliction architecture allowing integration and run-time reconfiguration of the various collision avoidance approaches. We also discuss the properties of the presented algorithms on empirical data provided by large scale experiments and we present the testing scenarios.

2. AGENTFLY System Architecture

AGENTFLY is fully written in JAVA, AGENTFLY can be easily hosted on assets with different operating systems. The multi-agent system for flight modelling consists of several components, see Fig. 1. AGENTFLY system can be started on a single dedicated computer or distributed in computer clusters without any specific reconfiguration.

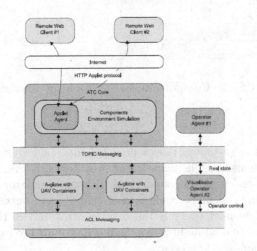

FIGURE 1. AGENTFLY System Structure Overview

Environment Simulation Components

The *components for environment simulation*, Fig. 2, of the AGENTFLY system is a sole central element of the system. It simulates positions of UAAs and other objects in the simulated world, aircraft hardware, weather condition, communication ranges given by the ranges of board data transmitters, etc. During the deployment of real UAA hardware these components will be removed and replaced by data

acquisition systems from real on board sensors hosted by UAA and the control
link will be redirected to the UAA's actuators.

One of the environment simulation components is responsible for acquisition
and fusion of information about all airplanes with freely available geographical
and tactical data sources. These are provided to both the *remote WEB client* and
the *operator agents*. There is also a *simulation scenario player* that controls the
simulation flow by e.g., creating new UAAs and providing them initial mission
specification (sequence of time specific way-points). Detailed information about
environment simulation components can be found in [8]. For the very extensive
simulations with hundreds of UAAs these components simulating the environment
can be split among several servers integrated by means of the *A*-**globe** *topic mes-*
saging concept.

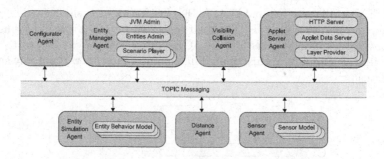

FIGURE 2. Components for environment simulation

UAA Containers

Each airplane in the system is represented by one *UAA container*, Fig. 3. The
container hosts two agents. The *plane agent* provides high-level airplane functions
such as flight plan execution in cooperation with the simulator component, radar
and detector readings, airplane configuration, time synchronization and operator
bridge interface. The *pilot agent* is the main control unit of the UAA. It has a
flight planning module a no-flight zones manager, a multi-layer collision avoidance
module and a human-agent interface.

Within one *A*-**globe** instance (one JVM process running *A*-**globe**) there can be
one or more such UAA containers. Such configuration allows to perform very large
simulations (scalability experiments) using more host computers. The AGENT-
FLY simulation component responsible for the UAA startup performs also load
balancing when deciding where the new UAA container will be created. One of
the future versions of *A*-**globe** will provide also dynamic load balancing using the
concept of container migration.

Remote WEB Client

The *remote WEB client* is an optional component of the AGENTFLY, Fig. 4.

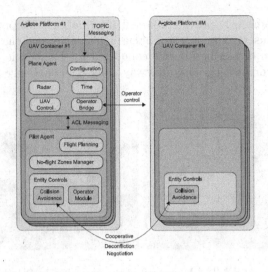

FIGURE 3. *A*-**globe** with UAA containers

It allows a remote user to display requested information which she needs. There is a secured authentication of the user. So each user can have different levels of information enabled. AGENTFLY has been integrated with real world data. External data are taken from public databases with various GIS data for the area of the United States – landsat images, state boundaries, airports, cities, highways and real civil traffic. The client connection is optimized to provide only needed data so it can be operated using slow network connection.

FIGURE 4. Web interface providing 2D view of the simulated area with integrated external data sources

Operator Agent

Real-time visualization of the internal system state in a 3D/2D environment is provided by the *operator agent*, Fig. 5. AGENTFLY allows running a number of such

agents who simultaneously provide different information with proper access level
rights to different users. The operator agent is also able send the user commands
back to the system or can be directly connected to the specific UAA container.
The user can then manage the aircraft's way-point plan or change defined no-flight
zones.

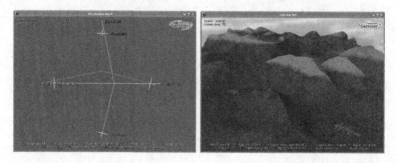

FIGURE 5. AGENTFLY system state provided in 2D (left) and
3D (right) view using operator agent.

3. Flight Planning in AGENTFLY

The inputs to the planner are (*i*) the list of waypoints (WP) (the coordinates
that the airplane must visit in specific times), (*ii*) the velocity, which the airplane
should have at the beginning of its route and (*iii*) repository with no-flight zones
(NFZ), which the plane must not enter during its flight and plan the path to avoid
them.

The planning of a flight path proceeds in two phases. In the first phase – *path
planning*, the planner generates the shortest flight plan, which passes through all
WPs avoiding the NFZs. In the next phase – *time planning*, some parameters of
the segments (mostly speed, but sometimes also the trajectory) are adjusted in
such a way that the modified flight plan satisfies the time constraints of the WPs.

NFZs represent an important concept for non-cooperative collision avoidance.
The presented algorithms work with three types of no-flight zones used in the ATC
system: (*i*) *world zones* – represent ground terrain and other static obstacles in the
simulated world, (*ii*) *static zones* – encapsulate world areas where UAV cannot
operate, e.g., enemy zones, and (*iii*) *dynamic zones* – hold zones which change
frequently, they are mainly defined by NFZ-based non-cooperative deconfliction
as described later. AGENTFLY supports various data structures for the no-flight
zones: octant tree [2], height maps and primitive objects – sphere, cylinder and
cube. All types can be combined together using grouping, scaling, translation and
addition/subtraction operations on them.

The path planning problem has been solved by the original *manoeuvre-based
path-finding* algorithm that is defined by two points (start, destination) and by two

vectors (initial direction, target direction). The manoeuvre-based algorithm incorporates a single A* progressive path planning [7] using basic flight plan elements with dynamic size of discrete steps.

Similarly to the algorithm of path planning, the time planning algorithm is based on particular elements' chaining. In case of path planning these elements were manoeuvres, in case of time planning these are time elements. In contrast to path planning, time elements are not expanded using algorithms for state space exploration (such as A*). Instead, they are only suitably chained one by one, with pre-calculated parameters. The time planning phases produce a plan for which the time of flight through each segment corresponds to the time constraints defined in the original planning problem specification.

4. Agent-Based Collision Avoidance Methods

The AGENTFLY system features a selection of different *cooperative collision avoidance* methods. Cooperative collision avoidance is a process of finding a mutually acceptable collision avoidance manoeuver among two or more cooperating flying assets. The assets are capable of mutual interaction and provide each other fully trusted information. They are optimizing their own interests (e.g., fuel costs increase, delays) with consideration of the interests of the colliding assets. Even though the concept of cooperation in the field of multi-agent systems implies optimization of the social welfare (sum of costs and utilities of all the involved parties), we understand the concept of cooperation in broader sense. We have developed and studied three different cooperative collision avoidance algorithms: *Rule based collision avoidance* (RBCA), *Iterative peer-to-peer collision avoidance* (IPPCA) and *Multi-party collision avoidance* (MPCA).

Besides cooperative algorithms, the AGENTFLY system also features *noncooperative collision avoidance* methods. The noncooperative collision avoidance algorithm operates an individual flying asset when facing a collision thread with a flying object that does not interact with the to-be-avoided asset or the asset is not trusted.

4.1. Rule-Based Collision Avoidance (RBCA)

RBCA is a domain dependent collision avoidance algorithm, which is based on the *Visual Flight Rules* defined by the Federal Aviation Authority (FAA)[1]. Each flying asset performs one of the predefined collision avoidance maneuver by means of the following procedure. First, the type of the collision between the airplanes is identified. The collision type is determined on the basis of the angle between direction vectors of the concerned aircrafts projected to the ground plane. Depending on the collision classification each UAA applies the collision avoidance manoeuvre from the set of defined rules. The manoeuvres are parameterized that they uses

---

[1]http://www.faa.gov

the information about collision and angle so the solution is fitted to the identified future conflict.

The above rule-based changes to the flight plan are done by both the assets independently because the second aircraft detects the possible collision with the first plane from its point of view. Substantial inefficiency of the RBCA algorithms is caused by the fact that the predefined visual flight rules perform collision avoidance without any altitude changes.

4.2. Iterative Peer-to-peer Collision Avoidance (IPPCA)

The *iterative peer-to-peer collision avoidance* algorithm is an extension of the pair optimization for multiple collisions among several UAVs based on utilities provided by themselves. The basic version provides a solution for a pair of colliding airplanes, see Fig. 6. The algorithm optimizes social welfare in that pair, thus the aircraft would like their flight plans to maximize the sum of their utilities, but still find collision-free paths.

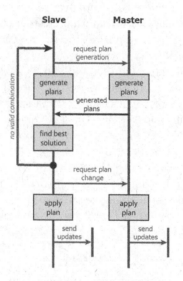

FIGURE 6. The negotiation during IPPCA

First, the participating airplanes in the colliding pair select the master and the slave part for the detected collision (usually the first entity which identifies a collision is regarded as a master entity). Each planning agent generates a set of new plans using the pre-defined parameterized collision avoidance manoeuvres. The flight plan modified by applying the manoeuvre includes its utility value which is composed as a weighted sum of several parts using the following equation:

$$u = \frac{\sum_i \alpha_i u_i}{\sum_i \alpha_i}, \tag{4.1}$$

where α_i denotes the weight for the i component of the utility function. The utility function is used for including the aircraft's intention in the proposed solution of the conflict and depending on the configuration it can contain different components to be taken into consideration, such as the total length of the flight plan, flight priority, fuel status and other factors. Seven parameterized changing manoeuvres can be used in the current version: *straight, turn left/right, turn up/down, speed up* and *slow down* changing manoeuvres. The parametrization is used during the generation process to obtain a wider range of solutions in a situation when the solution is not found using smaller changes.

The best possible solution is identified by the following algorithm. The master generates a combination of all the proposed plans (including the original one) and as a solution it selects a pair of plans for which the first collision occurs later than the collision currently being solved, and which has the best sum of the utility values of the plans used in the pair. When there are more pairs with the same sum value, the solution is selected randomly from these. Both sides (master and slave) then apply the selected solution. If there is no pair of plans fulfilling the condition that the first collision must occur later than the one being solved, it is necessary to generate more different flight plans using higher values of parameters describing the changing manoeuvres. The extension of the method for multi-collisions among several UAVs is in the iterative use of the described algorithm. To prevent infinite loops of iterations, the algorithm is restricted so that the UAV cannot generate such a change of the flight plan that would lead to a collision with an already de-conflicted aircraft occurring earlier than the currently solved collision. The second restriction is that an aircraft can apply only such changing manoeuvres that are not opposite[2] to those already applied within the same solving batch[3].

The same algorithm has be used for finding the collision-free paths for self-interested UAAs. Such assets do not optimize the social welfare but they try to reduce the loss from collision avoidance. The best possible collision avoidance pair is identified by a variation of the *monotonic concession protocol* (MCP) [17]. The MCP is a simple protocol developed by Zlotkin and Resenschein for automated agent-to-agent negotiations [19, 9]. Instead of iterative concession on top of the negotiation set the algorithm uses the *extended Zeuthen strategy* [18, 4] providing negotiation equilibrium in one step and no agent has an incentive to deviate from the strategy. The implementation selects randomly one of the pareto-optimal solutions which maximize the product of the utilities.

---

[2]The opposite changing manoeuvres are defined in the three groups: turn left/right, turn up/down and speed up/slow down.
[3]Solving batch is a chain of consecutive algorithm runs.

4.3. Multi-Party Collision Avoidance (MPCA)

The multi-party collision avoidance approach removes the iteration known from the IPPCA algorithm during multi-collision situation – a situation when more than two UAAs have mutual future collision on their flight plans. MPCA introduces *multiparty coordinator* who is responsible for the state space expansion and searching for optimal solution of multi-collision. The multi-party coordinator is an agent whose role is to find a collision free set of flight plans for a possibly colliding group of UAAs - the *multi-party group*. The coordinator keeps information about the group, state space tree, chooses which airplane will be invited to the group, requests UAAs in the group for generating deconfliction proposals or sends the information about found non-colliding flight plans, see Fig. 7. Note that MPCA algorithm is running while planes are flying. Thus time for finding the solution is limited.

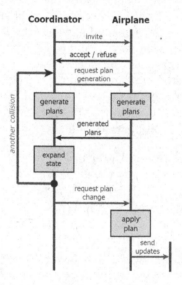

FIGURE 7. The negotiation during MPCA.

A coordinator agent is created by the master plane of the pair which detects future collision on their current flight plans. A master in the pair is determined according to alphabetical order of UAA's ids. When the coordinator is created it starts to search for a non-colliding set of flight plans. The collision which causes creation of a new coordinator is then treated as an *initial collision*. The searching algorithm proceeds in the three following steps which are repeated until a solution is found.

1. **Step 1** – The coordinator requests two planes from the group for possible flight plan changes to avoid their collision. Each of these planes individually

generates a set of changes and sends the partial plans back to the coordinator. Additionally, UAA checks for each avoiding manoeuvre, if it is colliding with other airplanes not included in the coordination group and adds a notification about it to the response.

2. **Step 2** – When the coordinator receives possible changes, it expands state space making their cartesian combination. Depending on the notification about external collisions the coordinator decides whether to invite (to enter the group) new UAA not already in its group which is colliding with the received changed flight plan. In the current version, the size of the coordination group is not restricted.

3. **Step 3** – The coordinator searches through combinations of generated flight plans. If the coordinator decides that more variants are needed, it continues with step 1. If it finds the final solution (a set of non-colliding flight plans), it sends message to planes from the group with their new flight plans.

The main part of communication during a session between the coordinator and a UAA is shown in the Fig. 7. The session starts with the `invite` message sent from the coordinator to an airplane. The UAA can respond with an `accept` or a `refuse` message. If the invitation is accepted, the UAA is added to the coordinator's multi-party group and the coordinator can request for plan generation when needed. If the parts of the flight plan that are used for detecting a collision are too short (the first collision point is identified but the last collision point cannot be found due to the short flight plan), the coordinator sends a request to the UAA for a longer part of its plan. Additionally a `failure` message can be sent in both ways. Failure can occur when the flight plan is changed for reason unrelated to the group, e.g., an asset can be forced to switch to a different type of a conflict avoidance method which can make the change of its actual flight plan causing a removal of the plane from the group. Another situation when a failure can happen is when an asset contained in one multiparty-group changes its flight plan due to its involvement in another multiparty-group .

The coordinator assumes that the initial plans in the group are not changed during the search. If flight plans change for some of the planes, such a plane is removed from the group. This plane can be added to the group upon new collision detection. This relates to the problem of concurrent existence of several coordination multi-party groups.

By default, the state space generated in the MPCA is searched by the A* algorithm with zero heuristics which is only admissible one [10] in our case – due to the allowed changing manoeuvres which do not change the utility value but can find a non-colliding solution. For example in the scenario where two UAAs have collision on their perpendicular flight plans and the utility value depends only on the flight plan length, the best solution is when one plane speeds up and another slows down having the same utility values as the initial state. There is a defined condition (too large state space and not enough time for searching optimal solution) when the used heuristics need to be switched to the non-admissible heuristic preferring expansion of states with less collisions. Such searching is then very fast, but its result is the less optimal solution.

4.4. Non-Cooperative Collision Avoidance Architecture

The path planning algorithms are used for planning individual flight plans (based on WP and NFZ) but also for non-cooperative collision avoidance replanning that is initiated once an aircraft detects a flying object. AGENTFLY uses the algorithm based on modeling the future possible trajectory of the opponent (the non-cooperative flying object) and dynamic encapsulation of its possible location by NFZ. NFZ is regularly updated after each radar update. Such implementation can be combined with another cooperative collision avoidance algorithm which uses the same identified dynamic NFZ.

The event that triggers the collision avoidance loop is information obtained from the radar describing the position of an unknown object in the area. This object is recorded in the base of non-cooperative objects, unless it's already present there. If the object is already known, its position is updated.

The next step is *prediction of the collision point*, an intersection of the flight plan and the non-cooperative object. If no such virtual collision point is found, the loop ends. In the opposite case, the collision point is wrapped by a dynamic no-flight zone. Such zone is then used for the test if the current flight plan intersects the zone and if the intersection is found, the path is re-planned.

The shape of dynamic no-flight zones of non-cooperative objects (Fig. 8) is derived from the possible future flight trajectory. The trajectory takes into account the minimal turning radius, maximal climbing and descending angle and the prediction time. We do experiments with dynamic NFZ with an ellipsoid shape which is not placed at the position of the observed flying object but at the place of the predicted collision and its size reflects the speed of the objects and the distance to the collision point.

FIGURE 8. Shape of the dynamic no-flight zone

The described non-cooperative collision avoidance loop is executed for all objects found in the radar scan. This is done periodically for each radar scan.

5. Multi-layer Collision Avoidance Architecture

The listed collision avoidance methods are linked by the *multi-layer collision avoidance module* [13] that is a part of a special planning agent, hosted by each of the UAA platforms. This module is capable of solving the future collisions by means of combination of different avoidance methods. There is no central planner providing a collision free flight plan, hence the individual plans are provided by the planning agents. The proposed modular architecture is domain independent. Therefore it is ready for deployment on autonomous vehicles like airplanes (UAA) or ground vehicles (UGV).

Multi-layer collision avoidance module hosts CSM (*Collision Solver Manager*), the main controller responsible for the selection of the CS (*Collision Solver*) that will be used for specific collision. CSM is able to combine all the available cooperative and noncooperative algorithms. The previously presented collision avoidance algorithms are implemented as plug-in solver modules and can be domain dependent or independent. Each collision solver is responsible for the collision detection (e.g., *Collision Point Prediction* in the non-cooperative CA or *Collision Detection* in cooperative CA) and collision registration with CSM. One collision can be detected by several collision solvers.

Based on priority, CSM assigns each registered collision solver a time slot that can be used for solving by the specific CS. The priority of the solvers is preset, but can be altered during the runtime. Concatenation of these slots creates time axis providing a specific, time-oriented switching among the CS operation. Sophisticated switching of the collisions solvers is inevitable in our application as the solvers have different properties. Different solvers provide different quality of the collision-free solution, while they require different amount of time for finding such solution. Specifically, the negotiation oriented solvers may provide better solution than non-cooperative solvers, while they may be more time consuming (given by the multi-party interaction). As the time is a very critical factor in our collision avoidance domain, some solvers are not guaranteed to terminate prior a possible collision.

6. Deployment Scenarios and Selected Experimental Results

In this section, the selected deployment scenarios, where presented algorithms were tested, are listed. The main criteria that the algorithm is stable and converges in many testing setups to the final solution is fulfilled by all the tested collision avoidance methods.

In the first scenario, the UAAs are located in a circular formation at the same flight level (altitude, referred to as FL). All of them want to fly to the opposite side of the circle through its center. Therefore there is a multi-collision of all the planes at the same time located in the center of the circle. The results after using distributed rule-based (RBCA) and iterative peer-to-peer collision (IPPCA) avoidance methods are shown in the Fig. 9. The RBCA has defined rules which

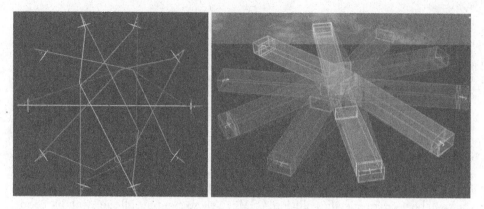

FIGURE 9. Scenario with 10 UAAs in the circle: The result for
RBCA 2D view (left) and IPPCA 3D view (right).

change the flight plan only in the same flight level. The result for RBCA is still
at the same FL. The IPPCA provides a solution that is substantially closer to the
optimum (almost 100 times shorter additional flight trajectory for the scenario
with 80 aerial assets - see Fig. 10. It uses six available avoiding manoeuvres (as
defined in the section 4.2). The graphics in Fig. 9 demonstrate higher compactness
of the IPPCA solution in comparison to the solution provided by RBCA.

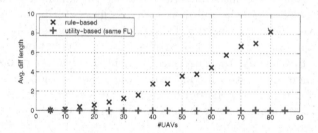

FIGURE 10. Scalability experiment: The comparison of the difference in the final flight plan length for the RBCA and IPPCA

We have defined an automatized experimental scenario setup which is used
for scalability testing. During the experiment run several characteristic properties
can be recorded and compared. The experimental environment uses the worst-case
setup. The UAAs are randomly generated on one of the four sides of the limited
experiment area. All of them need to fly to the opposite side. The entry point of
each new UAA is generated on adjacent borders in clock-wise direction. Both the
initial way-points entry and the exit are at the same FL. The setup provides the
high number of the future collisions in the central part of the testing square. The
plot in the Fig. 10 presents comparison of average (each setup was measured 50
times) sum of differences between the final deconflicted and the initial flight plan

for all the UAAs in the specific experiment run. For this experiment, IPPCA can use only four avoiding manoeuvres which do not change the flight altitude. The IPPCA provides solution much better than RBCA especially for the cases with more UAAs.

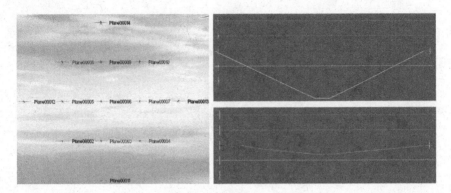

FIGURE 11. Wall scenario: Left: the setup of the experiment. Right: the result after IPPCA (top) and MPCA (bottom).

In the next scenario, there are 13 UAAs flying in a vertical plane in 3D. Their positions in the space are shown in the Fig. 11 left. All of them initially fly in the same direction at the same flight speed. There is another UAA which is flying in the opposite direction and has a potential to head collision with the UAA located in the middle of the first group. The final results comparing the IPPCA and MPCA algorithms are depicted on the right side of the same Figure. In the IPPCA version, only one plane performs a large detour of the group of UAAs and therefore no other planes participate in the solution. On the other hand, in the MPCA version, the middle UAA in the group performs a combination of several changing manoeuvres and creates a small hole in the middle of the group to let the opposite UAA fly through. Then the UAA goes back to its original relative (central) position within the group. The MPCA solution gives only 0.213 units longer solution than the initial plan while the IPPCA solution is 2.843 longer. The values were calculated as an average from 20 consecutive experiment runs.

The Fig. 12 displays the scalability experiment results comparing the IPPCA and MPCA algorithms. In this case both algorithms uses the same scenario setup and the same set of avoidance manoeuvres. Each run was measured 50 times to provide average result values for both the methods. The top plot in the Fig. 12 is the comparison of the final solution lengths. The MPCA algorithm gives a more optimal solution – depending on the number of UAAs, the results are improved by 10 to 50 percent compared to the IPPCA. The bottom chart is the comparison of total communication flow during the experiment run among all the UAAs. Both algorithms have almost the same amount of transmitted bytes, but we have identified that the flow distribution in time is different. The MPCA algorithm

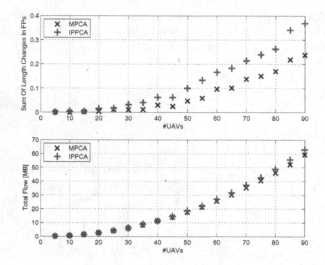

FIGURE 12. Scalability experiment IPPCA vs. MPCA: The sum
of differences between final collision-free paths and the shortest
regardless collisions (top). The total communication flow (bottom).

in the current version requires communication link bandwidth up to 600 kB per
second and the IPPCA needs only 50 kB/s.

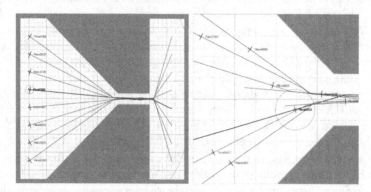

FIGURE 13. Tunnel scenario: Initial configuration (left) and the
collision avoidance result for IPPCA (right).

Another high density scenario is shown in the Fig. 13. There are eight UAAs
willing to fly from their starting positions through the small tunnel (the size of
safety zone around UAA is the same as the size of the hole) to their destination on
the right side. All UAAs fly at the same FL and they cannot manoeuvre and avoid
collisions by changing this altitude. Both algorithms IPPCA and MPCA solve

this situation. UAAs change their flight speed to accelerate before the hole and than they adjust the flight speed that all of them have the same flight speed. The result is shown in Fig. 13 right screen. Although UAAs can use the right and left manoeuvres they do not apply them because there is not enough space there. This case can be compared to a very intensive landing scenario, where several airplanes want to land at the same runway in a very short time interval, e.g., landing at an aircraft carrier.

type	average trajectory length $l[u]$		
	proportional navigation	dynamic NFZ	no control
perpendicular collision	33,21	33,85	30,0
slant collision	31,17	31,52	30,0
head-up collision	30,81	30,62	30,0

TABLE 1. Non-cooperative experiments with one controlled and one uncontrolled UAA comparing proportional navigation with the dynamic no-flight zones algorithm.

The non-cooperative algorithm (Section 4.4) has been compared with the optimization proportional navigation (PN), see [13] for more details. The PN algorithm provides a very good result when coping with a single alien flying object, but it cannot be extended to the situation with several non-cooperative objects located nearby. Moreover such optimization algorithm cannot be used in a combination with other cooperative methods at the same place. In the Table 1, there are the results of non-cooperative experiments with one controlled and one uncontrolled UAA. The uncontrolled UAA always flies directly from the starting point to the destination and the controlled one is always heading north and it must avoid collision in the middle of the operation area. Again no altitude changes are allowed to provide relevant comparison (PN doesn't support such changes). The results for both algorithms are almost the same. The PN provides better results in two setups and in the third one the dynamic NFZ gives a more optimal solution.

The Fig. 14 displays the minimal separation among UAAs with safety zone size highlighted in the scenario with two uncontrolled UAAs (obstacles). The PN was configured to take into consideration the nearest obstacle first. The PN algorithm fails to avoid the collision while the dynamic NFZ works properly in this situation. We have performed several other experiments with more UAAs, all using the described non-cooperative algorithm within a worst-case scenario. The method handles all situations without any collision.

The multi-layer collision avoidance architecture allowing combination of cooperative and non-cooperative methods at the same time has been validated in the deployment where real civil traffic operates over Los Angeles International

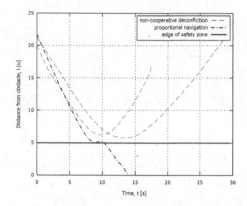

FIGURE 14. The distance from obstacle in the scenario with three UAAs, where only one uses active control non-cooperative avoidance method.

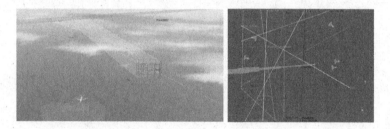

FIGURE 15. Operation of agent-controlled UAAs over LA with imported real air-traffic

Airport. There are two types of aircrafts in the setup. There are randomly operating agent-controlled UAAs which are configured to use the IPPCA algorithm with other UAAs controlled by agents. If there is another flying object identified they will use non-cooperative avoidance methods to solve the identified collision with it.

The simulated air-traffic is extended by real civil airplanes of which the dynamic positions are imported from publicly available internet sources. These airplanes are detected by on-board radars of the agent-controlled UAAs. The Fig. 15 provides both the 3D and the 2D view of the simulated area.

7. Conclusion

This chapter describes a possible use of agent technologies in the free-flight collision avoidance domain. We present a complex multi-agent system that provides a realistic air traffic simulation and a practical collection of different collision avoidance methods. A sophisticated switching architecture allows autonomous, decentralized, run-time selection of an appropriate deconfliction method based on current distances and velocities, traffic density and level of trust between the to-be-avoided closing objects. Extensive experiments demonstrated viability, efficiency and scalability of this approach.

The experimental verification of the efficiency of the negotiations among highly distributed autonomous assets did show clear convergence of all the proposed algorithms. Given the results shown in the previous section, it is clear that the rule based approaches are obsolete given the demonstrated performance of the iterative peer-to-peer negotiation protocols . However, the difference in performance between these and the multi-party collision avoidance is less evident.

All the scenarios presented as test cases here represent just the starting point of investigation of more complex cases where more UAAs and civil aircraft will be engaged, with a wider variety of permitted maneuvers, with sub-optimal communications and with more dramatic changes in the environment. This approach is inherently less constrained, and may allow for unanticipated emergent behaviors to arise, hence our emphasis on empirical testing. However, we feel we have clearly documented that our approach is robust and efficient, and definitely worthy of continued development.

The main potentials for further extensions of the AGENTFLY technology include e.g., collision avoidance among the collaborating assets with limited communication capabilities (so that the location of the asset is kept undisclosed), introduction of the mobile stand-in agents in the collision avoidance process (in order to minimized the required communication traffic), use of the collision avoidance architecture for implementation of various collective flight models or theoretical analysis of the convergence of the listed communication protocols.

Acknowledgement

AGENTFLY development has been sponsored by the Air Force Office of Scientific Research, Air Force Material Command, USAF, under grant number FA8655-06-1-3073. A-globe has been mainly developed under the grant numbers FA8655-04-1-3044 and FA8655-02-M-4057. The U.S. Government is authorized to reproduce and distribute reprints for Government purpose notwithstanding any copyright notation thereon. The views and conclusions contained herein are those of the author and should not be interpreted as representing the official policies or endorsements, either expressed or implied, of the Air Force Office of Scientific Research or the U.S. Government.

The authors wish to acknowledge help, assistance and inspiration of their collaborators Victor Skormin and John Beyerle.

Appendix A. $\mathcal{A}$-globe Multi-Agent Platform

AGLOBE[4] is a flexible and open multi-agent environment, which supports integration of heterogeneous distributed computational processes (agents). It is distributed under CPL licence[5]. $\mathcal{A}$-**globe** is different from existing multi-agent platforms' by:

- SCALABILITY - its emphasis on high efficiency of the computational process allowing scalability of multi-agent simulations,
- SIMULATION - support for modeling and simulation in of the environment in which the agents have been designed to operate,
- MIGRATION - full support of migration of the agents and computational processes in distributed environment, and
- VIZUALIZATION - $\mathcal{A}$-**globe** also provides sophisticated visualization support for design and testing of complex multi-agent systems.

$\mathcal{A}$-**globe** is a fast and lightweight platform with agent mobility and inaccessibility support. Besides the functions common to most of agent platforms it provides Geographical Information System-like service to the user. Therefore, the platform is ideally suited for testing experimental scenarios featuring agents' position, position dependent environment simulation and communication inaccessibility. The platform provides support for permanent and mobile agents, such as communication infrastructure, storage, directory services, agent migration (including library migration with version handling), service deployment, etc. $\mathcal{A}$-**globe** is optimized to consume just a limited amount of resources.

$\mathcal{A}$-**globe** platform is not fully compliant with the FIPA specifications; still it implements most protocols and respects the spirit of the specification. It does not support communication between different agent platforms (e.g., with JADE, JACK, etc.). For large scale scenarios the problems with system performance that interoperability brings (memory requirements, communication speed) outweigh any advantages, as heterogeneous environment is of limited interest for simulations. The $\mathcal{A}$-**globe**'s operation is based on several core components, see Fig. 16:

- Agent Platform that provides the basic components necessary to run one or more agent containers, the container manager and the library manager.
- Agent Container that is a skeleton entity that provides basic functions such as communication, storage and management for agents.
- Services that provide shared functions for all agents in one container
- Environment Simulator Agents that simulates the real-world environment and controls visibility among other agent containers
- Agents who integrate various computational processes, user interface or hardware components and represent basic functional entities in a specific simulation or control scenario.

---

[4]http://agents.felk.cvut.cz/aglobe/
[5]Common Public License Version 1.0 – http://www.opensource.org/licenses/cpl1.0.php

The agents have various means of communication. They can interact either via (i) standard ACL (Agent Communication Language) message passing, (ii) by topic messaging - specific simulation oriented messaging among containers, (iii) service sharing - where the agents can use or provide each other with various specific services.

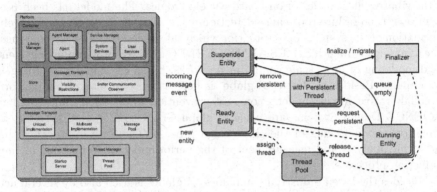

FIGURE 16. $\mathcal{A}$-**globe** platform architecture (left). Agent lifecycle (right).

The $\mathcal{A}$-**globe** platform is primarily aimed at large scale, real world simulations with fully fledged agents. To support this goal, it includes a special infrastructure for environmental simulation. Actor agents play roles in the simulated world, while Environment Simulation (ES) agents implement the simulated world itself. ES agents only rarely use messages to communicate with actor agents. Instead, they communicate via topic messaging. Topic messaging implements container to container messaging reserved for easy environmental simulation. Topic messaging is built on top of standard messages and is managed by the Geographic Information System (GIS) Services - server and clients. GIS services provide distribution and subscription mechanism for the agents. ES agents can be responsible for nearly any simulation layer, depending on the wishes of the developers. The accessibility agent, which controls the availability of communication links between containers holding the actor agents, is one of the most important of ES agents. $\mathcal{A}$-**globe** messaging layers use the information provided by the accessibility agent to prevent sending messages between inaccessible nodes. The accessibility simulated by the system can depend on many factors, typically including the distance and simulated link reliability.

$\mathcal{A}$-**globe** has been developed in the Gerstner Laboratory, Czech Technical University. Since its initial development in 2001 $\mathcal{A}$-**globe** has been successfully deployed in various industrial domains. Besides its chief deployment in Air Traffic control of unmanned aerial vehicles, described in this chapter, $\mathcal{A}$-**globe** has been also used for the simulation of underwater minesweeping operations, funded by the Office of Naval Research. Agents perform collaborative decision making aimed at intelligent surface search and sharing communication bandwidth when streaming high resolution images to the control base. The simulation has been successfully transformed to the robotic environment in order to prove its versatility. The robocup soccer robots were used for the hardware simulation of $\mathcal{A}$-**globe** based underwater minesweeping operation. Based on $\mathcal{A}$-**globe** the Gerstner Laboratory developed in cooperation with DENSO Automotive, GmBH an agent based system for distributed diagnostics of on-board car electronics. The model has been used for an operation failure root-cause-detection while also for the process of graceful degradation of the systems operation (for which safe regions of car electronics need to be dynamically identified). US ARMY CERDEC are currently supporting agent-based modeling of large scale computer networks, based on $\mathcal{A}$-**globe** multi-agent environment. Besides modeling, $\mathcal{A}$-**globe** is here used as an integration platform for collaborative intrusion detection and prevention application. The company CADENCE Design Systems are using $\mathcal{A}$-**globe** CE (CADENCE EDITION) for simulation and modeling of the chip design process. They use multi-agent simulation for analysis and measurement of the performance and efficiency of their production processes.

Besides the listed industrial companies, $\mathcal{A}$-**globe** is used also by several academic institutions: University of Edinburgh, Florida Institute for Human and Machine Cognition and Masaryk University.

References

[1] DOD. Unmanned aircraft systems roadmap 2005-2030, 2005.

[2] S. Frisken and R. Perry, "Simple and efficient traversal methods for quadtrees and octrees," *Journal of Graphics Tools*, 7(3), 2002.

[3] S. C. Han and H. Bang, "Proportional navigation-based optimal collision avoidance for uavs," in S. C. Mukhopadhyay and G. Sen Gupta, editors, *Second International Conference on Autonomous Robots and Agents*, pages 76–81. Massey University, New Zealand, 2004.

[4] J.C. Harsanyi, "Approaches to the bargaining problem before and after the theory of games: a critical discussion of zeuthen's, hick's, and nash's theories," *Econometrica*, (24):144–157, 1956.

[5] J. C. Hill, F. R. Johnson, J. K. Archibald, R. L. Frost, and W. C. Stirling, "A cooperative multi-agent approach to free flight," in *AAMAS '05: Proceedings of the fourth international joint conference on Autonomous agents and multiagent systems*, pages 1083–1090, New York, NY, USA, 2005. ACM Press.

[6] J. Krozel, M. Peters, K. D. Bilimoria, C. Lee, and J. S. B. Mitchel, "System performance characteristics of centralized and decentralized air traffic separation strategies," in *4th USA/Europe Air Traffic Management R & D Seminar*, Stanta Fe, NM, December 2001.

[7] N. J. Nilsson, *Problem-Solving Methods in Artificial Intelligence*. McGraw-Hill Pub. Co., 1971.

[8] M. Pěchouček, D. Šišlák, D. Pavlíček, and M. Uller, "Autonomous agents for air-traffic deconfliction," in Peter Stone and Gerhard Weiss, editors, *Proceedings of the Fifth International Joint Conference on Autonomous Agents and Multiagent Systems*, pages 1498–1505. ACM, 2006.

[9] J. S. Rosenschein and G. Zlotkin, *Rules of Encounter*. The MIT Press, Cambridge, Massachusetts, 1994.

[10] S. Russell and P. Norvig, *Artificial Intelligence: A Modern Approach*. Prentice Hall Series in Artificial Intelligence, Englewood Cliffs, New Jersey, 1995.

[11] T. Sandholm, *Multiagent Systems: A Modern Approach to Distributed Artificial Intelligence*, chapter Distributed Rational Decision Making, pages 201–258. MIT Press, Cambridge, MA., 1999.

[12] D. Šišlák, M. Rehák, M. Pěchouček, M. Rollo, and D. Pavlíček, "*A-globe*: Agent development platform with inaccessibility and mobility support," in Rainer Unland, Matthias Klusch, and Monique Calisti, editors, *Software Agent-Based Applications, Platforms and Development Kits*, pages 21–46, Berlin, 2005. Birkhauser Verlag.

[13] D. Šišlák, P. Volf, A. Komenda, J. Samek, and M. Pěchouček, "Agent-based multi-layer collision avoidance to unmanned aerial vehicles," In James Lawton, editor, *Proceedings of 2007 International Conference on Integration of Knowledge Intensive Multi Agent Systems*, volume KSCO 2007. IEEE, IEEE, 2007.

[14] C. Tomlin, G. Pappas, and S. Sastry, "Conflict resolution for air traffic management : A study in muti-agent hybrid systems," 1998.

[15] D. Šišlák, M. Rehák, M. Pěchouček, D. Pavlíček, and M. Uller, "Negotiation-based approach to unmanned aerial vehicles," In *DIS '06: Proceedings of the IEEE Workshop on Distributed Intelligent Systems: Collective Intelligence and Its Applications (DIS'06)*, pages 279–284, Washington, DC, USA, 2006. IEEE Computer Society.

[16] J. P. Wangermann and R. F. Stengel, "Optimization and coordination of multiagent systems using principled negotiation," *Journal of Guidance, Control, and Dynamics*, 22(1):43–50, 1999.

[17] S. Wollkind, J. Valasek, and T. R. Ioerger, "Automated conflict resolution for air traffic management using cooperative multiagent negotiation," in *Proc. of the American Inst. of Aeronautics and Astronautics Conference on Guidance, Navigation, and Control*, Providence, RI, 2004.

[18] F. L. B. Zeuthen, *Problems of monopoly and economic warfare*. Routledge and Sons, London, UK, 1930.

[19] G. Zlotkin and J. S. Rosenschein, "Negotiation and task sharing among autonomous agents in cooperative domains," in N. S. Sridharan, editor, *Proceedings of the Eleventh International Joint Conference on Artificial Intelligence*, pages 912–917, San Mateo, CA, 1989. Morgan Kaufmann.

David Šišlák, Michal Pěchouček, Přemysl Volf, Dušan Pavlíček, Jiří Samek and Vladimír Mařík
Gerstner Laboratory, Agent Technology Group
Czech Technical University, Department of Cybernetics
Czech Republic
e-mail: sislak@fel.cvut.cz

Paul Losiewicz
European Office of Aerospace Research and Development
Office for Scientific Research, US Air Force Research Laboratory
London
UK
e-mail: paul.losiewicz@london.af.mil

Whitestein Series in Software Agent Technologies, 97–112

Controlling Teams of Uninhabited Air Vehicles

Jeremy W. Baxter and Graham S. Horn

Abstract. We describe a Multi-Agent System (MAS) for controlling teams of uninhabited air vehicles (UAVs) in the context of a larger system that has been used to evaluate potential concepts of use and technologies. The approach is one of a decision-making partnership between a human operator and an intelligent uninhabited capability. The MAS controls the UAVs and self-organises to achieve the tasks set by the operator with interaction via a variable autonomy interface. We describe how the agents are integrated with the rest of the system and present a number of system integration issues that have arisen. The overall system has been evaluated in a number of human-in-the-loop trials within a detailed synthetic environment.

1. Introduction

Uninhabited vehicles can be used in many applications and domains, particularly in environments that humans cannot enter (e.g., deep sea) or prefer not to enter (e.g., war zones). Uninhabited air vehicles (UAVs) are of particular interest to the defence sector because they have the potential to significantly reduce the risk to aircrew in military operations. The promise of relatively low cost, highly reliable and effective assets that are not subject to the physical, psychological or training constraints of human pilots has led to much research effort across the world. Current systems, such as Predator or Global Hawk, require multiple operators to control a single platform. This chapter describes an approach to allow a single operator to control multiple platforms which has been evaluated in a number of human-in-the-loop trials within a synthetic environment (SE).

1.1. Concept

The concept is one of a decision-making partnership between a human operator and an intelligent uninhabited capability. The human provides mission-level guidance (with support from planning tools, etc.) to the "pool" of co-operating UAVs and takes on a largely supervisory role. The UAVs self-organise to achieve the goals set by the operator. Due to regulatory or liability issues, some critical decisions will have to be made by a human. Therefore, the uninhabited capability must refer such decisions to the operator. This concept has been implemented using a variable autonomy interface onto a multi-agent system, as part of a larger trials system.

The trials system is used to evaluate potential concepts of use and technologies. It is therefore nòt a static system but one in which different subsystems (such as different human machine interfaces) can be inserted and evaluated. SE based trials enable the key requirements for the decision-making partnership to be captured. The elements of the system have evolved in response to feedback from trials (subjective comments and objective performance measures) and changes to the concepts of use.

A multi-agent system (MAS) provides a natural and powerful way of representing multi-platform tasks and sets of coordinated and cooperating agents. Agents carrying out tasks which are clearly linked to a single platform can be hosted on that platform while more general purpose agents can spread out amongst the platforms. Planning systems can be integrated into the system by producing agents to wrap them.

1.2. Scenario

The scenario used for the trials was a time-critical targeting mission against a high value, mobile target. A package of four UAVs was deployed to locate and destroy the target. The operator was the pilot of a single-seat fighter, operating outside of the threat range of ground-based anti-aircraft defences. The UAVs are equipped with (long- and short-range) sensors and weapons. The mission consists of two main phases: search and attack. An example run is described in section 5.

1.3. Overview

The remainder of the chapter is structured as follows. First we describe how variable autonomy is achieved within the system. An overview of the trials system is given in section 3 before describing the multi-agent system (section 4) and how it is used to control and coordinate the UAVs. Section 5 describes an example run. Some of the issues we faced when integrating the MAS with the other components are highlighted in section 6, particularly the integration of deliberative planning systems with the reactive planning approach used by the agents. Finally we describe some results from the trials, some related work and conclusions.

2. Variable Autonomy

Variable autonomy is achieved by using the PACT framework [4]. PACT stands for Pilot Authority and Control of Tasks and incorporates a hierarchy of interaction between automated systems and an operator (such as a pilot), as shown in Fig. 1. At one extreme the operator decides (level 0), at the other the system decides (level 5), and in between are a number of "assisted" levels such as the system providing advice on request (level 1) or asking for permission to carry out a suggested decision

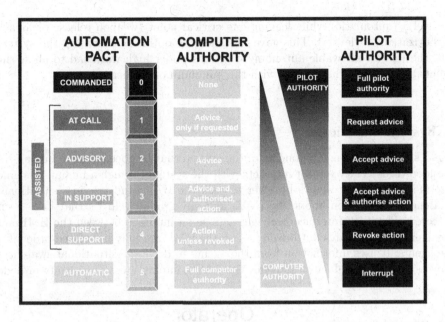

FIGURE 1. The PACT level designations.

(level 3). In the trials we have only used the highest three PACT levels, since the MAS is geared towards task execution rather than the provision of advice.

Key decision points, such as mission phase transitions, that may require operator approval trigger the agents to make PACT requests to the operator, via the Task Interface Manager (TIM). The operator can set the PACT level for each possible PACT request and these values are stored in the TIM. This provides a level of abstraction that means the agents will always send a PACT request and the TIM will determine whether or not to forward it to the operator. At PACT level 5, the TIM will immediately give approval and then inform the operator that the decision has been made. At PACT level 4 the TIM sends a message to the operator to inform him of the action that the agents intend to take and gives him a short time window to reject the request before the TIM will give approval on his behalf. At PACT level 3 the TIM (and hence the agents) must wait for the operator to approve or reject the request. The agents may also cancel a request if it is no longer appropriate, for example if a target they intended to attack is reclassified as destroyed.

In one of the trials the system was configured so that the pilot could define two different sets of PACT levels. These were defined as "minimum autonomy" (AMIN) and "maximum autonomy" (AMAX). The minimum autonomy level was typically set so that all PACT decisions were at level 3 (wait for authorization). This required the system to halt at each decision point until positive confirmation was made by the user. The maximum autonomy setting typically set most decisions to level 5 (automatic) while leaving one critical point (weapon release or attack authorization) at level 3. This gave the pilot the option of switching the system into the highest allowable autonomy if he was under high workload to allow the agents to carry out the mission with the minimum of further input.

3. System Overview

Fig. 2 shows the main components of the system that has been used in human-in-the-loop trials. The operator interacts with the system through a human-machine interface (HMI) that allows him/her to task the UAVs and provides situational awareness information about the UAVs and any ground vehicles that have been detected. The Task Interface Manager acts as an interface between the HMI and the agents. It translates button-presses on the HMI into fully populated orders for the agents. It uses information from the agents to drive the situational awareness aspects of the HMI. It also manages the PACT interactions. The agents provide

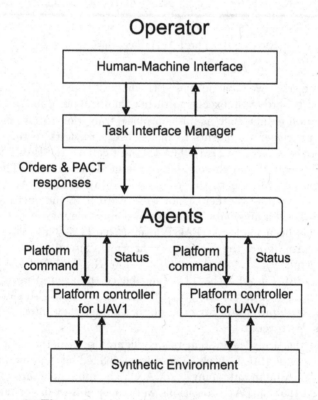

FIGURE 2. The main components of the system used in human-in-the-loop trials.

the self-organising system for controlling the UAVs which is central to the implementation of the concept. The agents send commands to controllers on each UAV platform and receive status and sightings information. The platforms exist inside a synthetic environment, which contains platform, sensor and weapon models, and different types of ground vehicles. Integrating all of these components has taken significant effort. Many components have been changed between the trials to investigate different aspects, such as the HMI design or type of weapon.

4. Multi-Agent System

The agents are structured as in Fig. 3. There are 4 types of agent. The User Agent acts as the conduit for tasking from, and information to, the operator. It allocates individual UAVs to tasks. The Group Agents are responsible for planning and coordinating the execution of tasks. Specialist planning agents are used to wrap a number of planning systems to allow them to be used by the agents. UAV agents interact directly with individual platforms, commanding the autopilot to undertake specific manoeuvres.

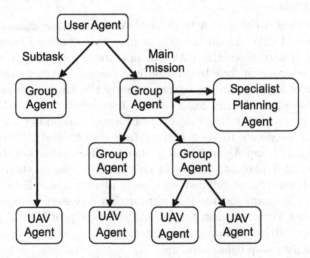

FIGURE 3. An example command and control hierarchy showing the different agent types.

The MAS was originally designed for controlling teams of entities in ground-based battlefield simulations. In its original form it only contained group agents and vehicle agents and did not allow an operator to issue new tasks during execution (a single order was provided to each team at start-up and this could be decomposed into orders for subgroups). The focus of the original work was on robust execution of these orders in the face of losses and failures [1]. The addition of the user agent allows for operator interaction and parallel tasking.

4.1. User Agent

The User Agent has control of all of the UAVs in the package. It accepts tasks from the operator (via the Task Interface Manager) and attempts to use the available UAVs to complete the tasks. The User Agent has a notion of a "Main mission" task to which all assets are assigned by default. The User Agent has full control over the task and may change the assignment of any of the UAVs involved in it. In addition to this default task, the operator may specify a number of "subtasks" which the User Agent is also responsible for trying to achieve. A subtask represents some specific action which the operator may require to be undertaken in addition to the default task, such as observing a specified location. The User Agent must select the assets to carry out each subtask. (In some trials the operator was able to specify which assets to use, if he so desired.) Once the User Agent has identified the UAV assets required for a task these assets are assigned to a Group Agent. Group Agents can be created by the User Agent or existing Group Agents can be re-used. The User Agent therefore controls a number of concurrent tasks on behalf of the user and uses the Group Agents to plan and supervise these tasks.

4.2. Group Agents

Group Agents exist to control a team of UAVs for a single task. Group Agents may either control UAV Agents directly or may control other Group Agents. For example, if a task requires the UAVs to operate in two pairs a Group Agent will control the group of four by tasking two Group Agents (each of these will control a pair of UAVs). Group Agents embody the knowledge of how to plan and execute coordinated team tasks using a framework (described in [1]) based on Joint Intentions theory [5]. This provides a solid grounding for the required communication necessary to keep a team task coordinated. Given an assigned task and assets a Group Agent makes a plan to achieve the task. It may call on additional specialist planning agents to do this. The plan is structured so that the roles which need to be fulfilled are clearly identified and UAVs are assigned to these roles. The plans include the coordination necessary to execute the plan. These plans then form the tasks for subordinate Group or UAV Agents and are sent to them for further planning and execution.

The primary group behaviours are:

- Search for a target, using short-range imaging sensors.
- Attack a target, combining weapon delivery and battle damage intelligence gathering.
- Search & Destroy, which combines the above two behaviours
- Fly a route in formation.
- Standoff search using long-range sensors.

4.3. Specialist Planning Agents

Two such agents have been used in our system.

4.3.1. Search Agent. The Search Agent provides access to a planner [9] that produces search routes. The planner is provided with a set of possible target positions and expands them into regions that could be reached by a moving target in the next few minutes. The search routes are designed to allow the UAVs to search these regions with short-range sensors and take images of potential targets that will be classified by the operator.

4.3.2. Attack Agent. The Attack Agent provides access to a dynamic scheduler [10] that allocates UAVs to the tasks that must be carried out during the attack phase: release the weapon and gather images of the target after the weapon has detonated to see if it has been destroyed. Typically two UAVs are available for these tasks, which may be split between them or one UAV may be chosen to undertake all tasks. The aim of the scheduler is to minimize the time taken to hit the target and get visual confirmation of its destruction.

The dynamic scheduler implements a deliberative planning process, derived from sequential decision theory, but specialised to weakly coupled systems (in which execution of tasks is decoupled after resource assignment) and with appropriate task models which could be used to plan a wide range of behaviours. The scheduler implements joint planning up to some time horizon, beyond which uncertainty in the scenario is expected to invalidate attempts to form longer-term plans. In scoring proposed plans, it makes use of task models to evaluate the effect (in terms of state, time and cost) of assigning particular resources (UAVs) to particular tasks. These task models can be stochastic (allowing for uncertain outcomes), but in this application only deterministic task models were used. The dynamic scheduling technology provides an upgrade path in which longer-term (tactical and strategic) considerations can be taken into account through the use of a value function that is evaluated at the planning horizon and added to the score of each plan. The value function can be hand-designed or acquired by trial-and-error learning in simulation (reinforcement learning).

4.4. UAV Agents

A UAV Agent exists for each UAV platform. It sends commands to the sensors, weapons and autopilot via a lower level platform controller. The UAV Agent monitors the status of the vehicle and sends sensor and state information to the other agents. The UAV Agents can plan and execute single vehicle tasks, such as taking images of a specified ground entity, and can try different actions until they achieve the tasks set by the Group Agent.

The primary vehicle behaviours are:

- Fly a specified route (possibly taking images of potential targets).
- Take an image(s) of a ground vehicle (fly into position to do so, if necessary).
- Loiter observing a ground vehicle using an imaging sensor.
- Search an area using long-range sensors.
- Release a weapon.

5. Example Run

This section describes a typical run of the system, highlighting the actions taken by the agents and the interactions they have with the operator. At the start of the run four UAVs are on a pre-planned ingress route heading for the last known location of the target. As they close the operator orders that a stand off search of the area should be conducted, using long-range sensors, to build up a picture of activity within the search area. The agents interpret this as a subtask from the main mission. The User Agent selects the two UAVs on the outer edges of the formation to perform this stand off search. Fig. 4 shows how the agents have re-organised to accommodate this new structure. The User Agent is controlling two Group Agents, one representing the pair carrying out the stand off search and the other representing the pair continuing the ingress. The operator then specifies the main mission to be "Search & Destroy" and the User Agent automatically selects the two remaining UAVs carrying out the ingress to perform this task. The Group Agent assigned to the "Search & Destroy" task identifies that since no target has been classified it should enter the "Search" phase and try to find one. This Group Agent initiates a Search Agent, which calculates appropriate search routes which are then sent to the UAV Agents to execute. These agents fly their assigned routes and gather images of potential targets that have been identified and tracked by the stand off assets. The agent organization for this phase is shown in Fig. 5.

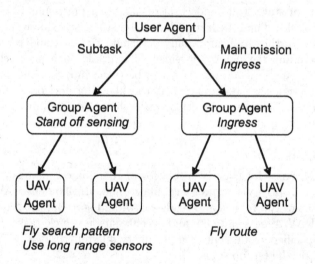

FIGURE 4. Agent organization for ingress and stand off sensing tasks.

When the operator has classified a ground entity as the high value target the agents infer that the search phase must be over and issue a PACT request, asking for permission to end the search and enter the attack phase. In this example we will assume the PACT level for this decision was set to be five, so the user

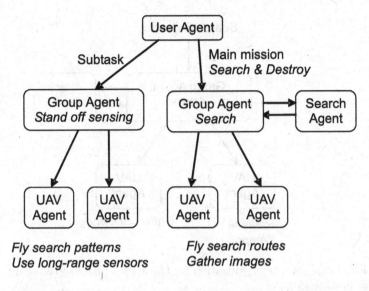

FIGURE 5. Agent organization during the search phase.

is presented with a message informing him that the search is over and that the package is entering the attack phase. The Group Agent now uses an Attack Agent to produce a plan, as shown in Fig. 6. In this example, one UAV is tasked to release the weapon and the other is tasked to gather battle damage intelligence (BDI) images after the weapon has impacted. When the first UAV is in position to release the weapon it issues a PACT request seeking final launch authorisation. This critical decision point has been set to level 3 and so the UAV cannot release the weapon until the user accepts the request. A timer is displayed on the HMI to indicate the launch window - if the operator does not respond before the launch window closes then the request will be withdrawn and the UAV will reposition itself before asking again. Assuming that the operator accepts the initial request promptly, the weapon is released. The BDI images are sent to the operator who confirms the destruction of the target.

6. System Integration Issues

Assembling the components for each trial has required significant effort. Compromises have had to be made to make things work given tight time constraints. This section highlights some of the issues faced when integrating the agents with other subsystems.

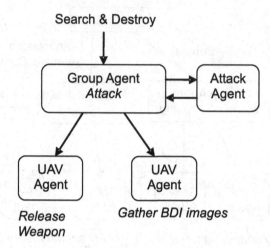

FIGURE 6. Agent organization for the attack phase of the search & destroy mission.

6.1. Reactive and Deliberative Planning

The agents are implemented using a Beliefs-Desires-Intentions agent language. We have built our own coordination framework on top of this to provide robust execution of group tasks. Group agents and UAV agents have sets of reactive plans to carry out group and individual tasks. Deliberative planning is done by the specialist planning agents. The search planner and the attack scheduler both contain models that are used to produce plans based on predicted future world states. Mixing deliberative and reactive planning can lead to problems. In particular, the task sequences produced by the scheduler are executed by UAV agents using reactive behaviours which differ from the models used for planning. This means that tasks may be completed in more (or less) time than expected and this may have a negative impact on the rest of the plan. Making use of the stochastic task models in the scheduler would provide better robustness to uncertainty in the outcome of actions. Closer integration of the deliberate and reactive elements would be helpful, such as sharing data structures (e.g., tasks, constraints, and plans).

Another issue is re-planning authority. The scheduler generates new plans on a regular basis, and when it finds one that is better than the current plan by some threshold the new plan is sent to the group agent in charge of the attack task. Currently, the scheduler does not take sufficient account of the cost of interruption and this can lead to delays rather than reducing the time to prosecute the attack.

The task sequences produced by the attack scheduler do not contain any coordination information (the tasks may contain preconditions based on time). Due to the number of different assignments that the scheduler might make (potentially all four UAVs might be available), we did not make full use of our coordination framework and fell into the trap of using an ad hoc coordination mechanism which was not sufficiently robust. Re-implementation to make use of our coordination framework was not possible in the time available before the trial which used the attack scheduler.

6.2. Communication

The trials system consists of a number of components (Fig. 2). These components have been developed by different groups in different programming languages. Interaction between the agents and other components, namely the TIM and platform controllers, is via XML messages over sockets. In the majority of cases we have used point to point client-server messages using TCP/IP. Whilst this is a verbose method of communication it has several important advantages over other message formats. XML messages are human readable, and this greatly assists debugging. It allows components to be easily replaced. The HMI and TIM used for the trials have been replaced with a ground control station without impacting the other parts of the system. In more recent work we have inserted an airborne radio link with its own compression and error handling protocols between the Agents and the HMI without having to change the existing interface. It is also easy to add new message types or to modify the message specifications. An earlier version used Java interfaces to separate the agents from the platform controllers, with the platform controller team providing implementations that would work with their component.

6.3. Logging and Debugging

In large distributed systems it is important to be able to understand what is happening (both during development and for post trials analysis) and to trace faults. Since the trials system is highly distributed each subsystem produces separate log files. The main log file generated by the MAS is an XML document which records all messages sent between the agents and "debug output" which provides information on which behaviours are being executed and values that they are using. This log shows how beliefs get propagated around the MAS. It is very difficult to maintain mutual belief and an important issue for future work is to look more closely at reasoning about when to send information to other agents.

We have written a tool to allow browsing of these files, and filtering of the information displayed according to the timestamp, message sender / receiver, message type, or "debug output" key / agent. The use of this tool has reduced the amount of time required to produce a summary of a run (including investigating potential faults) compared to using a text editor. An obvious issue is the accuracy of the timestamps. Every agent in the system has its own clock, which is set to a common time (based on the simulation time from a randomly selected UAV platform, accessed via the platform controller) at start-up. The initialisation of the agents does not take zero time, so these clocks will have some variation (less than a second, typically). This is an issue for any distributed system.

An example of the use of the logs for tracing faults is a problem that we had where the pilot was not receiving images that we thought should have been taken by the UAVs. Analysis of the MAS log showed that the UAV agents were not receiving notifications that images had been taken and in fact requests to take the images had not been sent to the platform controller, so the appropriate behaviour was modified to put the UAV into a better position in order to take an image of a ground vehicle. This fixed that part of the problem. Further analysis showed that the requests were now being sent to the platform controller but it was not sending them to the simulation because it had different values for the sensor field of view from those used by the agents and the simulation. When this was corrected we found that the images were taken, but sometimes the pilot did not receive them - due to an unreliable transport mechanism within the SE (an unexpected problem that thankfully did not occur often). Without our logging and support tools it would have taken much longer to identify and rectify these problems and they quickly justified the time and effort spent developing them.

6.4. Test Harness

Running the entire trials system requires a large number of resources (computers, people and time). In order to develop the agents separately we have produced a test harness which consists of a (lower fidelity) simulation and a number of displays (to replace the HMI and TIM). The test harness and the agents can be run on a single PC. The platform controllers and dynamics models are embedded within our simulation. The test harness has minimal start-up time, allowing a greater proportion of time to be spent testing behaviours and integrating the specialist planning systems. However, it is important to recognise the risk that behaviours may be prematurely optimised with respect to the test harness rather than the detailed synthetic environment.

7. Trials Results

7.1. System Performance

The multi-agent system has now been used in three successful human-in-the-loop trials. Results have shown that the approach is a good match to the concept of a human - intelligent system partnership. The pilots were able to successfully control a team of four assets to complete the missions. One of the problems in the first two trials was that the time taken to carry out the attack phase was too long, and this is why a separate attack scheduler was developed before the third trial. Fielding the system within a test and evaluation environment has revealed some implicit assumptions that the developers of different subsystems have made.

The PACT framework worked well when the pilots and agents were in agreement on the situation and the appropriate response. When the pilot refused a PACT request it was often unclear what the appropriate response of the system should be. For example, in some situations it might be appropriate to suggest an alternative, in others it might be appropriate to wait a short period of time and re-issue the same request. Usually the refusal of a PACT request indicates that there is a mismatch between the agents' assessment of the situation and the pilot's.

In the current system it is usually the case that a re-tasking by the operator has to follow a refused PACT request but future work plans to look at alternative ways of dealing with this problem.

7.2. Trust

One of the aims of this work is to reduce operator workload, so that a single operator can comfortably control a pool consisting of multiple UAVs, and one of the purposes of the trials is to investigate how much information is needed by the operator. A key requirement is a shared awareness between the operator and the intelligent capability about the current situation and what to do about it. The HMI must therefore enable the operator to understand what the agents believe the current situation to be and to provide the agents with the operator's view of the situation. The former is achieved through status reports that indicate the high level mode and objectives of the agents (which allow the operator to gain an understanding of the progress - at a suitable level of abstraction - of the tasks he has issued) and messages from the agents. Messages may be informative or alerts. Determining how many messages (and their priority) and the level of detail to show to the operator is difficult, because a terse system may be harder to trust, whereas a verbose system will overload the operator. Alerts can signal execution failures that the agents are unable to resolve without user assistance. The most recent trial has shown that these failures need to be communicated more clearly.

8. Summary

8.1. Related Work

The variable autonomy provided by PACT can be considered to be user-based adjustable autonomy as described by Maheswaran et al. [6]. The key decision points at which PACT requests are issued by the agents cover the two classes of policies in their framework, where a weapon launch request is an example of permission requirements for action execution and a request to advance the mission phase is an example of consultation requirements for decision making. Agent-based adjustable autonomy, where the agent decides when to transfer decision-making control to another entity, is not supported in our system.

Hierarchical architectures are an obvious choice for controlling uninhabited vehicles. Three examples follow. Howard et al. [3] present a three-layer model where the lowest layer (the action layer) is equivalent to the platform controllers in our architecture. Their single-agent layer is equivalent to our UAV agents. UAV agents, group agents and the user agent have aspects of their teamwork layer. Their hierarchical processing is instantiated by additional teamwork layer processes on some of the UAVs. These additional processes fill the role of the Group Agents and User Agent in our system. A bidding protocol is used to allocate tasks to UAVs or subgroups.

Chandler et al. [2] present a hierarchical agent architecture for controlling multiple vehicles. At the top is an inter-team cooperative planning agent which is equivalent to our User Agent. It uses an auction procedure to allocate observation targets to teams of UAVs. Below this are intra-team cooperative control planning agents (equivalent to group agents) which send tasks to vehicle planning agents (UAV Agents). At the bottom are UAV regulating agents which provide command sequences for the vehicle, control sensors, etc. (functionality provided in our system by UAV agents and platform controllers).

Vachtsevanos et al. [13] present a generic hierarchical multi-agent system architecture with three levels. Agents in the upper level mainly provide decision support tools for the mission commander, with a focus on global knowledge for producing team plans. Our group agents and specialist planning agents provide many of these functions. The middle level is responsible for planning and monitoring the tasks of a single UAV and is equivalent to our UAV agents. The lower level consists of a set of agents that control the vehicle, sensors, weapons, etc. and is designed to support heterogeneous UAV models. This functionality is provided in our system by the platform controllers (with some overlap with the UAV agents).

Our coordination framework (described in [1]) bears a close resemblance to the STEAM rules [11] (and the subsequent TEAMCORE work [12]) produced by Tambe et al., which is also based on Joint Intentions theory. The main difference is the presence of an agent representing the group as a whole that is responsible for instructing and coordinating the group members, as opposed to team members simultaneously selecting joint operators.

Miller et al. [7] describe a similar "pool" based approach where an operator (in this case an infantry commander on the ground) requests a service and the system attempts to provide it using available assets. They use a hierarchical task network planner, which is similar to the reactive plan decomposition used inside our group and UAV agents by default.

The Boeing Multi-Vehicle UAV Test bed [8] has controlled a team of small UAVs by using a combination of market based mechanisms for group co-ordination and evolutionary algorithms for path planning. We have experimented with a contract net protocol but have found that having an explicit group planner/coordinator gives better performance when the tasks are tightly coupled (for example requiring simultaneous observation by multiple vehicles prior to an attack by one of them). In general market based mechanisms work well when tasks are loosely coupled and the requirement is to spread the load over a set of available assets. In these cases we would expect a market based mechanism to scale better than the explicit team planning approach we have adopted.

8.2. Conclusions

The approach described in this chapter has been evaluated in a number of human-in-the-loop trials within a synthetic environment and it seems to be a good match for the concept of a decision-making partnership between a human operator and an intelligent uninhabited capability. The overall trials system provides a framework for evaluating concepts of use of potential technologies.

The multi-agent system is able to self-organise to achieve the tasks set by the operator. The PACT framework for variable autonomy worked well when the operator and agents were in agreement, but further work is needed to cope with cases where the operator rejects PACT requests.

References

[1] J. W. Baxter, and G. S. Horn, "Executing Group Tasks Despite Losses and Failures," in *Proceedings of the Tenth Conference on Computer Generated Forces and Behavioral Representation*, Norfolk, VA, 15-17 May 2001, pp. 205-214.

[2] P. R. Chandler, M. Pachter, K. Nygard, and D. Swaroop, "Cooperative control for target classification," in *Cooperative Control and Optimization*, edited by Murphey, R. and Pardos, P. M., Kluwer Academic Publishers, May 2002.

[3] M. Howard, B. Hoff, and C. Lee, "Hierarchical Command and Control for Multi-Agent Teamwork," in *Proc. of the 5th International Conference on Practical Applications of Intelligent Agents and Multi-Agent Technology (PAAM2000)*, Manchester, UK, April 2000.

[4] S. L. Howitt, and D. Richards, "The Human Machine Interface for Airborne Control of UAVs," *2nd AIAA Unmanned Systems, Technologies, and Operations Aerospace, Land, and Sea Conference and Workshop*, September 2003.

[5] H. Levesque, P. Cohen, and J. Nunes, "On Acting Together," in *Proc. of the Eighth National Conference on Artificial Intelligence (AAAI-90)*, Boston, MA, AAAI, Menlo Park, CA, 1990, pp. 94-99.

[6] R. T. Maheswaran, M. Tambe, P. Varakantham, and K. Myers, "Adjustable Autonomy Challenges in Personal Assistant Agents: A Position Paper," in *Agents and Computational Autonomy: Potential, Risks and Solutions*, edited by M. Nickles, G. Weiss and M. Rovatsos, Springer-Verlag, 2004.

[7] C. A. Miller, R. P. Goldman, H. B. Funk, P. Wu, and B. B. Pate, "A Playbook approach to variable autonomy control: application for control of multiple, heterogeneous unmanned air vehicles," in *Proc. of the 60th Annual Forum of the American Helicopter Society*, Baltimore, MD, June 7-10, 2004.

[8] A. Pongpunwattana, R. Wise, R. Rysdyk, and A. J. Kang, "Multi-Vehicle Cooperative Control Flight Test," in *Proc. of 25th Digital Avionics Systems Conference*, Oct 2006, IEEE/AIAA.

[9] M. J. A. Strens, "Learning multi-agent search strategies," *The interdisciplinary journal on Artificial Intelligence and the Simulation of Behaviour (AISB)* 1(5), 2004.

[10] M. J. Strens, and N. Windelinckx, "Combining Planning with Reinforcement Learning for Multi-Robot Task Allocation," in D. Kudenko et al. (Eds): *Adaptive Agents and MAS II*, Lecture Notes in Artificial Intelligence 3394, Springer-Verlag Berlin Heidelberg, 2005.

[11] M. Tambe, and W. Zhang, "Towards flexible teamwork in persistent teams," in *Proc. of the International conference on multi-agent systems (ICMAS)*, 1998.

[12] M. Tambe, W. Shen, M. Mataric, D. Goldberg, J. Modi, Z. Qiu, and B. Salemi, "Teamwork in cyberspace: Using TEAMCORE to make agents team-ready," in *Proc. of AAAI Spring Symposium on Agents in Cyberspace*, 1999.

[13] G. Vachtsevanos, L. Tang, and J. Reimann, "An Intelligent Approach to Coordinated Control of Multiple Unmanned Aerial Vehicles," in *Proc. of the 60th Annual Forum of the American Helicopter Society*, Baltimore, MD, June 7-10, 2004.

Acknowledgment

This work was funded by the research programme of the United Kingdom Ministry of Defence under contract DTA 3e 201.

Jeremy W. Baxter and Graham S. Horn
QinetiQ Limited
Malvern Technology Centre
St Andrews Road, Malvern, WR14 3PS
UK
e-mail: jwbaxter@QinetiQ.com
        ghorn@QinetiQ.com

Whitestein Series in Software Agent Technologies, 113–130

Simulating Fighter Pilots

Clint Heinze, Michael Papasimeon, Simon Goss, Martin Cross and Russell Connell

Abstract. Since 1990 a focused intelligent agent research and development programme within the Defence Science and Technology Organisation (DSTO) has underpinned a strong history of deployed operational simulations. Originally aimed at improving simulations of fighter pilots the research has expanded to include: fundamentals of agent languages and architectures; the cognition of teams; intention recognition and cognitive modelling; simulating civilian behaviour in conflict; intelligent environments; software engineering; and autonomy and uninhabited aerial vehicles. Capitalising on this research are a series of deployed simulations that have provided strong examples of the benefits of the technology. This paper presents a brief account of four successful agent-based simulation systems and a broad but shallow overview of some of the more interesting aspects of our relevant agent research and development activities.

1. Thinking Quickly and Clearly

The use of intelligent agent technologies[1] and methodologies[2] has reduced simulation development time and improved confidence and trust in results by facilitating subject matter expert validation—at least in the domain of air combat simulations built for operations analysis. Air combat is complex, adversarial and high-tempo. Fighter pilots, as military decision-makers, tend to follow procedures, are highly trained, exhibit high levels of expertise and are rational and predictable—at least within the context of the highly uncertain and unpredictable environments in which they function. Simulations that the Defence Science and Technology Organisation develops for analysing air operations require models of fighter pilots and other aircrew to pilot simulated aircraft through virtual battlespaces. Consideration of issues such as: pilot-to-pilot variability; sub-cognitive and physiological

---

[1]PRS, dMARS, JACK and other agent languages
[2]Agent UML, Agent Oriented Software Engineering and other agent based analysis and design approaches

effects; and other human factors like fatigue and currency of training are typically excluded simplifying the issue somewhat. The simulated fighter pilot must make sense of the simulated world, reasoning about appropriate courses of action and implement that course of action through the adoption of standard operating procedures and tactics. Two decades of related research and development have led to a suite of agent-based simulations built to meet this challenge [2, 31, 32].

Two primary advantages of the particular agent technologies that have been adopted for simulating fighter pilots are claimed:

1. that the AI or agent component of simulation can be developed more *quickly*; and
2. that the AI component of the simulation can be explained, understood and validated more *clearly*.

DSTO provides timely operational advice to the Australian Defence Force (ADF) about questions that might arise within the ADF specific to air operations and systems. This means that there must be a capability to answer a variety of questions and to analyse a wide range of scenarios. Analysts may be called upon to model, to a high degree of sophistication the physical systems (aircraft, radars, missiles, etc.) but must also be able to use these models within a scenario that is capable of simulating their tactical use and the interactions between them. A simulation will typically involve many aircraft, ground-based radars (GBR), missiles, electronic counter measures (ECM), and a variety of other systems. A critical requirement is that the simulations also model the pilots who fly the aircraft, air defence controllers who assist those pilots, and other human operators within the scenario. The models of the human operator should be capable of being modified rapidly whilst the behavior that they exhibit must be explainable in terms that can be understood and accepted as valid by those interested in the output of the work.

Within this context analysts provide advice with respect to:

- Capability analyses in support of the Defence acquisition process.
- Assistance with tactics and doctrine development for the effective employment of Defence assets.
- Advice for the development of training procedures for pilots and controllers at the operational level of command.

Military analysts use simulation to evaluate the effectiveness, performance, and tactical employment of military systems prior to acquisition or upgrade. The information that results from these studies guides acquisition and can be used to evaluate successive designs, thereby mitigating some of the risks associated with the physical development of modern defence systems. This type of simulation can also provide data for the evaluation of tactical options for situations that cannot easily be explored by conventional exercises or experimentation.

The modeling and simulation undertaken for the operations analysis activities of DSTO are largely *constructive*—without human interaction. This distinguishes it from the view of military simulation as the basis for human-in-the-loop training simulators where the emphasis is on providing an immersive environment. Constructive simulation places requirements on the intelligent agent development that are quite different from the computer generated forces found in training simulators [4]. An obvious difference is the requirement for real-time performance in human-in-the-loop systems whereas constructive simulations are usually required to run "as fast as possible". In practice this often means many times faster than real-time.

In training simulators the quality of the outcomes is frequently judged by the fidelity of the images presented to the human participant. As long as the entities appear to behave correctly the detail of the internal modelling is not questioned. This is not true of operations research simulations where the result is the accumulation of knowledge about the functioning of the hardware or the efficacy of particular tactics. In these cases it is necessary to develop a detailed understanding of the reasons for observed behaviours and a more explicit representation of the human component, and the tactics in particular [7]. It is for this reason that approaches that make clear the detailed functioning of the agent model are preferred. These simulators provide the human participant with an immersive visual and auditory experience that allows them to practice procedures and tactics. Agents have been used to provide both friend and foe in both training and operations research simulators [5, 6].

Despite flourishing research interest agents are relatively immature in industrial applications. The innovations that agents bring to software development require engineering methodologies that deal with concepts and techniques that differ from existing approaches. The immaturity of agents is reflected both in the small number of commercially available agent languages and the lack of supporting software engineering methodologies. Agents, as the term is used in this chapter, refers to a particular class of heavyweight agents that implement the BDI model operationalised in languages like PRS, dMARS or JACK [33, 34, 13].

2. Agents in Deployed Simulations

Our first intelligent agent project was a technology demonstrator that utilized the Procedural Reasoning System (PRS) from Stanford Research Institute (SRI). This technology demonstrator exhibited two qualities that proved decisive in transitioning to an operational system. The PRS programming language allowed coding of tactical plans in a fashion that supported rapid responses to suggested modifications. It was comparatively easy to develop and modify sophisticated tactics. Perhaps even more significant was the graphical nature of the plan language. PRS plans are flow-chart like representations of decisions. With careful design these can be made to resemble the types of decision trees that pilots draw when explaining their tactical decision-making. Clearly there were benefits to be had beyond simple software engineering maintainability that went to the very core of the promise of agent technology. These agents appeared to offer an appropriate level of abstraction and a set of modeling constructs that were ideally suited to the requirements. The following sections provide some details of some indicative projects that have made use of intelligent agents.

2.1. F/A-18 Hornet

SWARMM was a large and very sophisticated simulation of fighter combat. Agents were used to model combat pilots of different types and with different tactical repertoires. In defining a scenario, the analyst assigns high level mission plans to the appropriate agent team on the basis of their tactical role and mission assignment. Without any stimulating trigger the agent flies the mission as briefed, just as in real life.

In addition to the high level mission plans, the agents are assigned a suite of tactical plans commensurate with their role and mission in the scenario. Deviation from the pre-briefed mission behaviour is part of the central interpretive reasoning that considers the current state of the environment within the tactical context of the current mission phase. The plans are divided into a number of groups, of which the most significant is that dealing with manoeuvres. Other categories of tactics are those handling the operation of sensors, communicating, and weapons and countermeasures employment. Agents respond to events in the environment with tactics selected from one or more of these groups. SWARMM's tactical repertoire has been steadily developed within operational study requirements, in line with the original scope to provide a comprehensive suite of tactics commensurate with existing Air Force procedures.

The initial SWARMM project was successfully completed in June 1996 and further developments have matured its use as a tool for operational analysis. Planned as a progressive development project, SWARMM was heavily reliant on the content of previously developed models of aircraft and their systems. These models of aircraft and engine performance, weapons, countermeasures and environment comprise validated code that was developed by many staff over a period spanning more than a decade. The design concept of SWARMM foresaw the next stage of development being a move to an object-oriented (OO) environment for the physical systems modelling.

SWARMM was designed to alleviate, or avoid altogether, many of the problems associated with developing pilot tactics using traditional scientific code developed using languages like FORTRAN and C. To this end, the language used for simulation of tactical reasoning was dMARS (distributed Multi-Agent Reasoning System) and, in part, the SWARMM requirements specification influenced the development of dMARS as a C++ refinement of its LISP based precursor, PRS. SWARMM's dMARS employment of Beliefs, Desires and Intentions (BDI) agent formalism was an apt method of encapsulating the descriptions of human reasoning required in the domain of military air operations. The BDI approach enables the operational analyst to consider agent behaviour at the tactical level and to

FIGURE 1. Visualisation of an F/A-18 Hornet flown by a simulated fighter pilot implemented by a dMARS intelligent agent in
one of DSTO's air combat simulations.

map analyst operational experience into an appropriate set of tactical dMARS
plans [34, 32].

The tactics are written with respect to individual agents, or teams of agents.
Teams are broken into lead and wing elements and corresponding team plans re-
curse down to the individual lead and wing aircraft [35]. A typical agent would
have several thousands of these plans.

2.2. Airborne Early Warning and Control

During the down-select for the provision of an Airborne Early Warning and Control (AEW&C) aircraft to the Royal Australian Air Force simulation was used by
analysts as a tool to evaluate the characteristics of the tendered options. Within
this simulation agents were used to model the crew of the AEW&C aircraft and
other simulated entities that populated the scenarios of interest. The emphasis of
operational analysis studies in support the AEW&C projects was initially on the
evaluation of comparative hardware solutions sufficient to achieve proper operation

of the equipment under evaluation, in the way test pilots are used in trials of hardware systems. Relationships between agents were very formalised and simplified and required only simple agents with shallow command and control structures. The behavior required of these first agents was merely the operation of the aircraft in a tactically reasonable manner consistent with the aims of the tender evaluation. The crew of an AEW&C aircraft is required to perform a large number of disparate but complementary tasks. An AEW&C team is an information gathering, interpretation and dissemination centre as well as fulfilling a battle management role. Simulations are now moving to multi-agent systems that have depth in both command and control structure and in time. The depth of command and control structure requires that agents be capable of packaging and delegating tasks to those agents that have the capability to understand the requirements, read the situation, and carry out the intention of the delegating agent. These delegating agents must in turn be capable of understanding the intention of the agent above them in the command control structure in the tasks delegated to them. Another requirement is multi-agent systems that have depth in time. By depth in time we mean the ability of an agent to progressively gather an understanding of the situation over a period of time, infer the probable intention of those forces that are under its direct control and project the situation forward in time. With the AEW&C aircraft about to enter service the focus has moved away from analysis and evaluation of aircraft that are to be acquired and is now centered on support to the air crews that will operate the aircraft when it enters service. This has yielded a version of the simulation with the agents removed and in the place an interface that allows the real air crews to experiment with the tactical employment of the aircraft. The most positive aspect of this project was the capacity of Air Force operational personnel to participate in the coding of the agent representations using the dMARS language. This was facilitated by the graphical plan language of dMARS and a carefully designed agent reasoning architecture based on Col. John Boyd's observe-orient-decide-act (OODA) loop [37].

2.3. Strike Tactics

An agent oriented approach to modelling tactical decision making does not necessarily imply the use of agent oriented programming languages such as those based on the BDI model. Often agent languages such as dMARS and JACK are too heavyweight a solution when the tactical behaviour that needs to be modelled is simple. This was the case in the requirement to develop tactical procedures and concepts of operations for stand-off weapon strike missions undertaken by the Royal Australian Air Force's F-111 long range strategic strike aircraft. This involved modelling and simulating an F-111 aircraft (with associated sensors and long range weapons) flying through complex terrain in order to strike a high value target that was protected by ground based air defence systems. In this particular study, the tactical behaviour that needed to be modelled for the F-111 pilot and weapon systems officer as well as the enemy air defence officers was sufficiently straight forward so that sophisticated agent programming languages were not required. However, an agent-oriented approach was taken to capture and specify the requirements and for the design of the architecture for the agents. The actual implementation of the agent made use of standard object oriented tools and techniques using a finite state machine model to encode the tactical behaviour, similar to the approach taken to developing the artificial intelligence for video game characters. This approach allowed for the benefits of the agent-oriented paradigm to be used in the requirements and design phases of the project, while at the same time providing the simplicity, ease of development, lower risk and computational performance required for the implementation phase of the project.

2.4. Maritime Surveillance

This project supports the RAAF Maritime Patrol Group in developing new tactics and concepts of operation for the upgraded AP-3C Orion Maritime Patrol Aircraft. These are used in peacetime for maritime search, surveillance and intelligence gathering operations in and around Australian territorial waters. BattleModel is used to baseline the expected mission performance of the aircraft in typical mission profiles and scenarios, and also to develop new, integrated flying and sensor employment policies that allow the aircraft to function at its full potential. Here a model of the tactical decision making process on board the aircraft that was capable of representing the actual human operator and crew workload, the sensor data-fusion process and chain of command was needed. The tactical decision making model also had to be flexible and robust enough to allow timely modification to investigate different operational procedures and tactics. Individual dMARS intelligent agents were used to model the tactical decision making for each crew member being simulated on board the AP-3C. Intelligent agents were chosen because of the requirement to model decision making based on a degree of awareness of the environment or tactical situation the aircraft finds itself in. Maritime surveillance tactics, as with almost all tactical decision making, rely on making an assessment of the current situation based on fusing data from different sensors and also on making some assessment about the intent of other entities in the environment. The Beliefs, Desires, Intention formulation of the dMARS agents lends itself to this type of modelling. Crew members were modelled to the extent that the type of information, the amount of information and the work responsibilities of the operators were accurately represented. The simulation can operate in one of two modes; constructive or crew-in-the-loop. In the constructive mode, missions are run faster than real time, hundreds of times using monte-carlo techniques analysing the effectiveness of different tactics using statistical techniques. In this case, the tactical decision-making is made by the agents. In the crew-in-the-loop mode, the agents are removed from the simulation and are replaced with user interfaces which are controlled by actual crew members who make the tactical decisions. The interactive or crew-in-the-loop mode is used to test and evaluate new tactics in a realistic environment. In this mode, the tactical picture is projected onto a large screen showing the current sensor information which is superimposed on to a geographical map of the region. This allows the crew to focus on developing and evaluating higher-level tactical procedures rather than on low-level interactions with individual controls. A tactics development cycle involving the use of the constructive simulation with the intelligent agents, and the crew-in-the-loop exercises, is used to iteratively develop tactics and CONOPS over a period of time.

This process has proved very effective in combining the inputs of operational RAAF personnel and DSTO operations analysts to develop AP-3C tactics and CONOPS.

3. Agent Research and Development

From the early 1990s DSTO pioneered the employment of intelligent agent technologies in military operations research simulators. Through a series of successful collaborations with local academic institutions and technology vendors DSTO has been able to influence the direction of technology growth through involvement at all levels of agent technology research and development. A strong research and development program is continuing.

3.1. Agent Languages

DSTO's demanding requirements have driven the development of agent technology. DSTO played a major role in the development of dMARS both as an alpha and beta tester of the language and as a co-developer of methodologies, tools and language extensions. As users we played a larger role: developing some of the largest and most complex agent applications yet deployed. dMARS is a multi agent architecture that implements a BDI model of agency based on the concepts of intentions, plans and practical reasoning developed by Bratman [9]. Further information about the underlying formalism of dMARS is available [10, 11]. Every dMARS agent comprises a set of beliefs, desires (goals), plans and intentions.

The beliefs of an agent are stored in a relational database and contains information about the nature of the world. These beliefs may refer to hard physical data or to more abstract concepts. The goals of an agent are descriptions of required behaviors or desired outcomes, whilst the plans are declarative procedures specifying actions to take to accomplish these goals. The intentions are instances of plans that have been selected for processing to achieve some goal. They represent commitments by the agent to the achieving of a goal through the course of action specified by the plans. The plans represent the most visible part of a dMARS agent. They constitute the procedures that an agent will use to deal with situations as they arise. The plans are graphical in nature (see Fig. 2) and are capable of being displayed during the simulation through the dMARS Control Interface (DCI). This feature is an attribute of dMARS and not of agents per se; it allows the plans adopted by the agent to be displayed and the current state of the agent reasoning evaluated during the simulation. With careful design these plans can be read and understood by lay-people with little or no additional explanation.

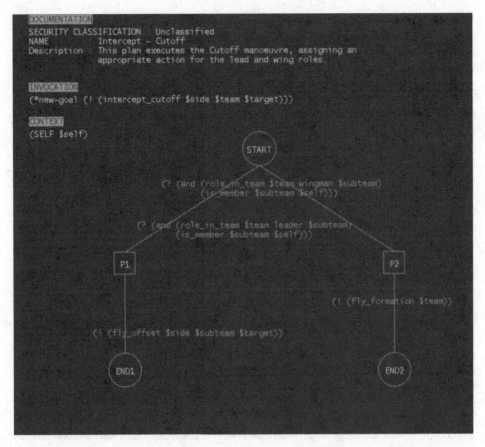

FIGURE 2. An example of a dMARS plan represented in the graphical plan language.

A detailed description of the dMARS system as it pertains to air-combat modeling can be found in [12]. A more recently developed alternative to dMARS is JACK [13]. JACK is based on Java and like dMARS implements a BDI model and provides many of the same programming constructs. DSTO actively cooperated in the development of extensions and supporting infrastructure for JACK and has collaborated in the development of several important extensions and additions to JACK [38].

3.2. Teams and Command and Control

Modelling teams and command and control has been identified as an important prerequisite for many of the future simulation based studies that are likely to be required. Increasingly, in military circles there is an emphasis on joint activities where all services cooperate to achieve more effective and efficient operations. With modern systems there is increasingly a need for the commander to understand the possible arrangements of assets that are available in order to assemble the best possible fighting force for a particular mission. Simulations in support of the innovative employment of teams and the flexible use of command and control must provide facilities for the explicit modelling of these concepts [16, 17].

3.3. Intention Recognition

In some of the earliest recorded descriptions of combative human behaviour it was noted that recognising the intent of an opponent was vital for success. Two and a half thousand years later intention recognition is still one of the most important aspects of military decision making and is significant in many other competitive and cooperative human endeavours. The simplest explanation for the need for recognition of intention lies in an inability or unwillingness to communicate. If someone is both willing and able to communicate fully and honestly about their intent then there is little need for recognition. If communication is unavailable, unreliable, or in the case of combative or competitive environment, undesirable then a mechanism for deducing the intent of others is required. In virtual environments recognition of intention is potentially as important as it is in the real world. This is due to both the proliferation of heterogeneous computer systems, networks, and agents that speak different languages, or because of security or resource constraints are unable or unwilling to communicate and there are applications that might benefit from computer systems capable of inferring human intent. Research is being undertaken into the provision of intention recognition capability for agents in simulation [18, 30].

3.4. Software Engineering

The employment of agent technology in SWARMM was one of the earliest steps in improved software engineering practices in model construction as it decoupled the reasoning models from the models representing physical systems. The Battle-Model architecture took this a step further enabling all models to be completely decoupled from each other, each model being highly cohesive, in an object oriented framework. Basically this meant that each model whether it be a radar, platform, missile, or reasoning model was independent and communicated with each other via the BattleModel architecture, enabling a plug-and-play type of simulation. Furthermore, it allowed for agent reasoning models of different fidelities and types to interact in the same simulation. For example, heavyweight BDI agents written in dMARS could interact with lighter weight reasoning models implementing a variety of techniques written in languages such as C++ and Java. The move to an agent friendly architecture led to research into how agent oriented systems should be engineered. To date this has involved looking at a number of different approaches including research into how existing object oriented methodologies such as the Unified Modeling Language (UML) [19] could be adapted or modified for agent oriented systems. Whereas agent researchers such as Odell and others looked at issues representing agent communication in UML through the use of

AUML (Agent-UML) [20], the research conducted looked at requirements specification, analysis and detailed design of agent systems. This included looking at how to extend the UML's concept of use cases for requirements specification of a system from a user's perspective, to one of behavioural specification of an agent system from an agent's perspective [21]. Furthermore, with the adoption of newer BDI agent languages such as JACK, design methodologies to support these new languages are required. Again an approach taken was to look at what existing techniques such as the UML could offer. Since JACK is a superset of the Java programming language with agent oriented extensions, and UML can be used to design Java programs, a logical approach would be to extend the UML to enable the modeling of JACK agents [22].

3.5. Computer Generated Forces

Our work reported here is largely concerned with constructive simulation but for certain applications above there are good reasons for involving flight crews directly in the simulation (the AP3-C development described above). There is the potential for intelligent agents to become an integral part of the human-in-the-loop facilities and they already are a promising part of studies into distributed mission training and distributed simulation in general. Throughout the world intelligent agents have been used as computer generated forces in HIL facilities (see Fig. 3) and insights into the problems that beset them have been gained from the experiences with agents in constructive simulation. Many of the issues associated with situating agents in simulations can be addressed in applications outside of the military domain. By examining the requirements on the environments that suitably support agent activity insights for military simulation development are gained. Another thread of research is exploring the addition of the principles of naturalistic decision making (NDM) to agents [26].

3.6. Autonomous Aircraft

A small but successful project modified the agent architectures used for simulating fighter pilots so that they would provide autonomous control of a light tactical uninhabited aerial vehicle (UAV). This project had the goal of investigating approaches for the implementation of autonomous tactical UAV control. The aircraft shown in Fig. 4 flew several missions as individuals and in teams.

3.7. Intelligent Environments for Intelligent Agents

An important lesson learnt from the deployment of many large intelligent agent based simulations was that complex tactical behaviour could not be developed in isolation as stand alone agent reasoning models. The environment in which the agents were situated in, and how the agents interacted with that environment was critical. This interaction became increasingly important not only because the requirements for tactical behaviour became more complex, but also because the environment (physical, social, command and control) in which air operations were being undertaken was becoming more sophisticated.

FIGURE 3. A Human-In-The-Loop F/A-18 Hornet Flight Simulator.

This lead to the development of an additional thread to the research program which focused on the virtual environments in which the intelligent agents were situated. The primary aim was to investigate techniques and approaches for designing and building meaningful virtual environments which were amenable to intelligent agents and which facilitated complex tactical behaviour. The investigation relied on theories from situated cognition and ecological psychology to inspire the design of the virtual environments and the agent-environment interaction [36].

Specifically the theory of affordances from ecological psychology was used as a basis for developing a more sophisticated model of agent-environment interaction. This interaction model was successfully implemented in a sophisticated simulation of a close air support (CAS) mission known as the Human Agent Virtual Environment (HAVE) [26]. A screenshot from this virtual environment is shown in Fig. 5.

3.8. Civilian Modelling

Complex terrain includes complex physical terrain, complex human terrain and complex informational terrain. Current military simulations and wargames rarely model complex human terrain and there are even fewer examples that include complex informational terrain and as combat within complex terrain becomes the norm civilian modelling becomes more important [29]. To represent civilians embedded

FIGURE 4. The Codarra Avatar was fitted with a HP IPAQ running a JACK agent connected serially between the radio modem and the flight control system. The agent provide autonomous control of the UAV: monitoring the aircraft state via the data sampled from the flight control system and controlling the aircraft through waypoints fed into the flight control system.

within a complex human and informational terrain a multi agent paradigm was selected as being the most appropriate due to the ability to incorporate different aspects of human behaviour and interaction in a visible structured manner.

Agents as members of social networks moving through their city from home to work is the first step this project has taken. This small step has none the less provided enough complexity to simulate disease spread through the population with results that replicate those provided by mathematical models such as SIR [28]. Initial extensions to these agents will increase the number of activities they undertake and allow reasoned responses to changes in their environments. Follow on research will explore emotion, motivation and the effect of cultural backgrounds on behavioural representation.

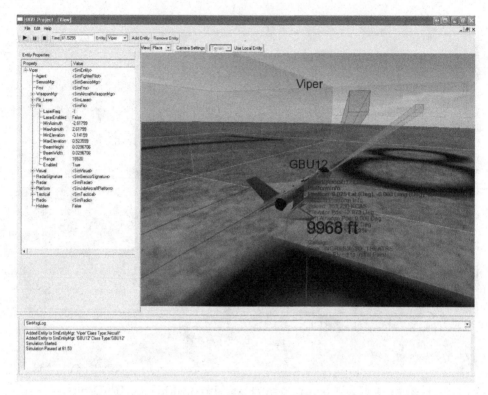

FIGURE 5. A screenshot from the Human Agent Virtual Environment (HAVE), a close air support (CAS) simulation. The design of the agent-environment interaction was motivated and inspired by the theory of affordances from ecological psychology; the study of how humans and animals interact with their environments.

4. Conclusions

The impact of intelligent agents within the DSTO can be measured in the successful deployment of a number of innovative systems, the associated productivity improvements resulting directly from the technology and indirectly from the associated adoption of improved software engineering practices, and the quality of the research that has been fostered in and around the development. In summarising the advantages of agents it is worth first cautioning that the particular adopted technology matched neatly with the requirements of defence science and though the application development has been successful it has not been without risk, steep learning curves, and cost. As Wooldridge and Jennings caution "There are a number of good reasons for supposing that agent technologies will enhance the ability of software engineers to develop complex distributed applications" but agents are not a magical problem solving paradigm [27].

By creating an environment where tactics and standard operating procedures are more explicitly represented it has been possible to improve the interactions between analysts and military personnel. The abstract graphical representation of plans provides the flight crews with visibility into the simulation increasing their confidence in the modelling. It allows tighter faster validation of tactical plans by inspection of crews and therefore improves the confidence that analysts have in the models.

Transitioning to agent technology shifted the focus from a systems view of military operations to a human centred view. This allowed problems to be viewed in radically different ways, for new research threads to be explored and for collaboration with psychologists, physiologists, and human factors experts to explore modelling options.

The acquisition of intelligent agent technology has resulted in large gains in productivity. Problems that were previously intractable have been opened up and explored while other problems are now addressed more effectively and efficiently. The particular implementations and technologies described here are clearly not suitable for all problems in all domains and care must be exercised when selecting novel technologies.

The particular domain and challenges facing the defence science meshed ideally with the adopted agent approaches and the significant risks associated with new technologies were mitigated through iterative development, careful tool acquisition and a firm research base. The success of a decade of intelligent agent research has resulted in quality outcomes for the Australian Defence Force, both in timeliness and quality, and an internationally recognised research program for DSTO.

References

[1] D. McIlroy, B. Smith, C. Heinze, and M. Turner "Air Defence Operational Analysis Using the SWARMM Model," in *Proc. of Asia Pacific Operations Research Symposium*, 1997.

[2] C. Heinze, S. Goss, T. Josefsson, K. Bennett, S. Waugh, I. Lloyd, G. Murray and J. Oldfield, "Interchanging Agents and Humans in Military Simulation," in *Proc. of Thirteenth Innovative Applications of Artificial Intelligence Conference*, Deployed Application Case Study Paper, Seattle, Washington, 2001.

[3] G. Tidhar, C. Heinze, S. Goss, G. Murray, D. Appla, and I. Lloyd, "Using Intelligent Agents in Military Simulation or "Using Agents Intelligently"," in *Proc. of Eleventh Innovative Applications of Artificial Intelligence Conference*, Deployed Application Case Study Paper, Orlando, Florida, 1999.

[4] M. Tambe, R. M. Jones, J. E. Laird, P. S. Rosenbloom, and K. Schwamb, "Building Believable Agents for Simulation Environments: Extended Abstract," in *Collected Papers of the SOAR/IFOR Project*, Information Sciences Institute, University of Southern California, pp. 78-81. Marina del Ray, CA, 1994.

[5] M. Tambe, K. Schwamb, and K. S. Rosenbloom, "Building intelligent pilots for simulated rotary wing aircraft," in *Proc. of the Fifth Conference on Computer Generated
Forces and Behavioral Representation*, pp. 39-44, 1995.

[6] D. McIlroy, C. Heinze, D. Appla, P. Busetta, G. Tidhar, and A. Rao, "Towards
Credible Computer Generated Forces," in *Proc. of Second International Simulation
Tech-nology and Training Conference, (SimTecT '97)*, Melbourne, Australia, 1997.

[7] C. Heinze, B. Smith, and M. Cross, "Thinking Quickly: Agents for Modeling Air
Warfare," in *Proc. of Australian Joint Conference on Artificial Intelligence, AI '98*,
Brisbane, Australia, 1998.

[8] R. L. Shaw, *Fighter Combat - Tactics and Maneuvering*. 6th edition, US Naval Institute Press, 1985.

[9] M. Bratman, *Intentions, Plans, and Practical Reason*. Harvard University Press,
Boston, MA, 1987.

[10] M. d'Inverno, D. Kinny, M. Luck, and M. Wooldridge, "A formal specification of
dMARS," in M. P. Singh, A. Rao, and M. J. Wooldridge, editors, *Intelligent Agents
IV* (LNAI Volume 1365), Berlin, Germany: Spinger-Verlag, 1997, pp. 155-176.

[11] M. P. Georgeff, A. L. Lansky, "Procedural Knowledge," in *Proc. of the IEEE Special
Issue on Knowledge Representation*, vol. 74, pp. 1383-1398, 1986.

[12] D. McIlroy and C. Heinze, "Air Combat Tactics in the Smart Whole AiR Mission
Model," in *Proc. of First International Simulation Technology and Training Conference, (SimTecT '96)*, Melbourne, Australia, 1996.

[13] N. Howden, R. Ronnquist, A. Hodgson, and A. Lucas, "JACK Intelligent Agents:
Summary of an Infrastructure," in *Proc. of the 5th International Conference on
Autonomous Agents*, 2001.

[14] G. Tidhar, M. Selvestrel, and C. Heinze, "Modelling Teams and Team Tactics in
Whole Air Mission Modelling," in *Proc. of Eighth International Conference on Industrial and Engineering Applications of Artificial Intelligence and Expert Systems,
(iea-aie '95)*, Melbourne, Australia, 1995.

[15] J. R. Boyd, *A Discourse on Wining and Losing*. Unpublished set of briefing slides
available at Air University Library, Maxwell Air Force Base, Alabama, 1987.

[16] G. Tidhar, "Organization-Oriented Systems: Theory and Practice," in *Department
of Computer Science and Software Engineering*, 1999, University of Melbourne: Melbourne, p. 278.

[17] R. Hodgson, R. Ronnquist, and P. Busetta, "Specification of Coordinated Agent
Behavior (The SimpleTeam Approach)," in *Workshop on Team Behavior and Plan
Recognition, International Joint Conference on Artificial Intelligence*, Sweden, 1999.

[18] C. Heinze, S. Goss, and A. Pearce, "Plan Recognition in Military Simulation: Incorporating Machine Learning with Intelligent Agents," in *Proc. of Workshop on Team
Behavior and Plan Recognition IJCAI' 99*, Stockholm, Sweden, 1999.

[19] G. Booch, J. Rumbaugh, and I. Jacobsen, *The Unified Language User Guise*. Read-
ing, MA: Addison Wesley, 1999.

[20] J. Odell, H. V. D. Parunak, and B. Bauer, "Extending UML for Agents," in *Proc. of
the Agent-Oriented Information Systems Workshop at the 17th National conference
on Artificial Intelligence*, 2000.

[21] C. Heinze, M. Papasimeon, and S. Goss, "Specifying Agent Behaviour With Use Cases," in *Proc. of Pacific Rim Workshop on Multi-Agents*, 2000.

[22] M. Papasimeon and C. Heinze, "Extensions to the UML for Designing Jack Agents," in *Proc. of the Australian Software Engineering Conference (ASWEC)*, Canberra, Australia, 2001.

[23] G. S. Halford, W. H. Wilson, and S. Phillips, "Processing capacity defined by relational complexity: Implications for comparative, developmental, and cognitive psychology," accepted as target article: *Behavioral and Brain Sciences*.

[24] C. Heinze and S. Goss, "Human Performance Modelling in a BDI Agent System," in *Proc. of OZCHI*, Sydney, Australia, 2000.

[25] R. M. Jones, J. E. Laird, "Constraints on the design of a high-level model of cognition," in *Proc. of Nineteenth Annual Conference of Cognitive Science*, pp. 124-132, 1997.

[26] M. Papasimeon, A. Pearce, S. Goss, C. Heinze and T. Patterson, "The Human Agent Virtual Environment," in *Proc. of 2007 Joint Conference on Autonomous Agents and Multi-Agent Systems*, Honolulu, Hawaii, USA, 2007.

[27] M. Wooldridge and N. Jennings, "Pitfalls of Agent Oriented Development," in *Proc. of the 2nd International Conference on Autonomous Agents (Agents '98)*, New York 1998. ACM Press.

[28] A. Skvortsov, R. Connell, P. Dawson and R. Gallis, "Epidemic Spread Modelling: Alignment of Agent-based Simulation with a SIR Mathematical Model,"

[29] Complex Warfighting Edition Two. ADF Future Land Operational Concept (FLOC) document.

[30] C. Heinze, *Modelling Intention Recognition for Intelligent Agent Systems*. PhD Thesis, Department of Computer Science and Software Engineering, University of Melbourne, Melbourne, Australia, 2003.

[31] C. Heinze, B. Hanlon, M. Turner, K. Bramley, J. Rigopoulos, D. Marlow and K. Bieri, "The ARTEMIS Air-to-Air Combat Model," in *Proc. of SimTecT '04, the Simulation Technology and Training Conference*, Canberra Australia, 2004.

[32] D. McIlroy, B. Smith, C. Heinze, and M. Turner, "Air Defence Operational Analysis Using the SWARMM Model," in *Proc. of Asia Pacific Operations Research Symposium*, 1997.

[33] J. Lee, M. J. Huber, P. G. Kenny, and E. H. Durfee, "UM-PRS: An Implementation of the Procedural Reasoning System for Multirobot Applications," in *Proc. of the Conference on Intelligent Robotics in Field, Factory, Service, and Space (CIRFFSS)*, Houston, Texas, 1994, pp. 842–849.

[34] M. d'Inverno, D. Kinny, M. Luck, and M. Wooldridge, "A formal specification of dmars," in *Intelligent Agents IV: Proceedings of the Fourth International Workshop on Agent Theories, Architectures and Languages*, number 1365 in Lecture Notes on AI, Springer, 1998, pp. 155–176.

[35] G. Tidhar, C. Heinze, and M. Selvestrel, "Flying Together: Modelling Air Mission Teams," in *Applied Intelligence*, vol. 8, pp. 195-218, 1998.

[36] M. Papasimeon, *Intelligent Environments for Agents*. PhD Thesis (in preparation), University of Melbourne, 2007.

[37] J. R. Boyd, "A discourse on winning and losing," Technical report, Air University, Maxwell AFB, Alabama, USA, 1987.

[38] N. Howden, J. Curmi, C. Heinze, S. Goss, G. Murphy, "Operational Knowledge Representation: Behaviour Capture, Modelling and Verification," in *Proc. of the Eighth International Conference on Simulation Technology and Training (SimTecT '03)*, Adelaide, Australia, May 2003.

Acknowledgment

The authors would like to thank the large number of air combat analysts, engineers and scientists who have contributed to the agent research and development programme over the last two decades.

Clint Heinze, Michael Papasimeon, Simon Goss, Martin Cross and Russell Connell
506 Lorimer St
Fishermans Bend, Victoria 3207
Australia
e-mail: clinton.heinze@dsto.defence.gov.au
        michael.papasimeon@dsto.defence.gov.au
        simon.goss@dsto.defence.gov.au
        martin.cross@dsto.defence.gov.au
        russell.connell@dsto.defence.gov.au

Whitestein Series in Software Agent Technologies, 131–150
© 2007 Birkhäuser Verlag Basel/Switzerland

MAS Combat Simulation

H. Van Dyke Parunak

Abstract. Multi-agent systems offer a new stage in the evolution of combat simulation. Originally, warfighters simulated combat manually to explore alternatives and plan their campaigns. The first applications of computers to combat simulation used algorithms that aggregated the warriors on each side, such as differential equations or game theory, effectively modeling the entire battlespace with a single process. Entity-based models such as OOS and Combat XXI assign a single agent to each entity, following the standard MAS agenda. A new modeling construct, the polyagent, takes this trend one step further, and uses several agents to model each construct. This approach addresses several challenges that face the traditional MAS approach, including fitting, closure, dynamism, and singularity. This chapter surveys the history of combat modeling, gives two examples of polyagent systems (one for planning, the other for adversarial prediction), and discusses how this construct addresses the challenges.

1. Introduction

Combat modeling is a discipline with a long history. Documented instances date at least to the Prussian Kriegsspiel of 1811 [34], but as long as humans have gone to war, fighters have systematically thought through the contingencies of actions and counter-actions in preparation for military operations (cf. Joshua 8:3-8; 2 Samuel 10:9-11). It is tempting to speculate that the model soldiers found in Egyptian tombs from 2000 BC [7] may have been inspired by implements for military experimentation. Combat simulation seeks to anticipate how an engagement may unfold and to assess the value of actions that the commander may take in each contingency. In the face of incomplete knowledge about the present, lack of access to the adversarys plans about the future, and the element of chance in every interaction, precise planning is impossible, but modeling can help warriors anticipate the range of possible outcomes. Traditional simulation methods fall into two

This chapter draws on previously published articles embodying research by several members of our group, including Steve Brophy, Sven Brueckner, Bob Matthews, and John Sauter.

categories: mathematical models and behavioral emulation. Mathematical models include the Lanchester differential equations, which relate force strength to attrition, and game theory, which models a forces comparison of its gains relative to those of its adversary across different options. Behavioral emulation simulates the movements of units and observes their interactions and the resulting outcomes. This emulation can be done with real troops in an exercise, with models on a sand table, or most recently with software agents in a simulated world.

Agent-based models of combat pose a number of challenges, which can be addressed by a novel modeling construct, the polyagent. The fundamental idea of the polyagent is to represent each domain entity by a plurality of software agents. A single avatar manages multiple ghosts, which explore alternative possible behaviors of the entity. As the ghosts of different avatars interact with each other, the system concurrently explores many possible interactions far more efficiently than could be done with distinct simulations involving only one agent per domain entity. We have used the polyagent model both to produce action plans, and to predict enemy intent. Section 2 reviews the major types of computational combat models that have been used over the last century, to provide a context for agent-based models. Section 3 describes the polyagent construct and two problems to which it has been applied (action planning and adversarial prediction). Section 4 shows how this approach addresses the challenges of conventional combat simulation and identifies a number of directions for future expansion.

2. Combat Modeling

The roots of combat modeling go back well before the computer era, and follow two distinct lines, one mathematical and the other behavioral.

2.1. Mathematical Models

Mathematical models of combat are of two main types: Lanchester theory and game theory.

Lanchester Theory. In 1916, F.W. Lanchester published a set of differential equations that expressed how the change in strength of each side in a conflict varies with the current strength of the other side [11]. In their simplest form, his equations define the evolution through time of the strength of the two sides, $R(t)$ and $B(t)$, as a function of the effective firing rates α_R and α_B of the two sides, $dR/dt = -\alpha_B B(t); dB/dt = -\alpha_R R(t)$. His system is a version of the Lotka-Volterra equations for predatorprey populations [35]. An early application of computers to military modeling was integrating the Lanchester equations, and many of the militarys leading models today are still based on refinements of this model, for example, the Bonder-Farrell Attrition Algorithm equations [2].

Game Theory. Game theory was originally developed in context of economic analysis [31, 32], but after WWII, it became a central tool for military planning at the DoD-sponsored RAND Institute and elsewhere. Game theory focuses on the rationality of the parties in conflict, and assumes that each seeks to maximize its own utility while recognizing that the other party is seeking to do the same.

Game theory and Lanchester theory differ in two important ways.

1. Lanchester theory models combatants as physical forces with no rationality. Game theory assumes that players are rational and seek to maximize a utility function.
2. Lanchester theory describes the evolution of combat through time. Game theory in its simplest form is concerned with the final outcome.

In spite of these differences, the two mathematical theories treat the opposing sides as aggregates, and do not consider the detailed interactions of individual soldiers and their weapons.

2.2. Behavioral Models

Behavioral models are exemplified by wargames, either with real troops or on sand tables on which experimenters alternatively move playing pieces to explore tactics (Fig. 1). Inexpensive computers and multi-agent techniques permit models of combat in which each entity is represented by an individual computer agent. Such models are superior to traditional mathematical models because they can capture the individual evolution of interacting entities, rather than modeling them as averages over the population. Combat interactions are strongly nonlinear, and population averages often miss important divergences in individual trajectories [27, 36]. As a result, entity-based models can often yield more realistic results than do Lanchester or game-theoretic models.

FIGURE 1. A physical combat simulation using a "sand table".

A disadvantage of agent-based models is that they can require more computation than classical mathematical models. Fortunately, relatively simple entity models, embedded in an environment based on cellular automata, are often sufficient to capture much of the complexity of warfare [9]. One explanation for this outcome is the phenomenon of universality [21], which recognizes that the structure of interactions may overwhelm differences in the processing carried out by individual agents.

For instance, EINSTein [9] represents an agents personality as a set of six weights, each in [-1, 1], describing the agents response to six kinds of information. Four of these describe the number of living friendly, living enemy, injured friendly, and injured enemy troops within the agents sensor range. The other two weights relate to the models use of a childhood game, capture the flag, as a prototype of combat. Each team has a flag, and seeks to protect it from the other team while simultaneously capturing the other teams flag. The fifth and sixth weights describe how far the agent is from its own flag and its adversarys flag. A positive weight indicates that the agent is attracted to the entity described by the weight, while a negative weight indicates that it is repelled.

MANA [12] extends the concepts in EINSTein. Friendly and enemy flags are replaced by the waypoints being pursued by each side. MANA includes four additional components: low, medium, and high threat enemies. In addition, it defines a set of triggers (e.g., reaching a waypoint, being shot at, making contact with the enemy, being injured) that shift the agent from one personality vector to another. A default state defines the personality vector when no trigger state is active. In spite of their simplicity, EINSTein and MANA yield highly realistic aggregate battle dynamics.

2.3. Unmet Challenges

Entity-based models, of which multi-agent models are an instance, offer significant benefits over mathematical models. But as implemented in current simulation technology (such as Combat XXI [1] and OOS [30]), they still face significant challenges. Four merit our attention.

Fitting. Having a separate agent for each unit or soldier allows the model to capture the effects of nonlinear interactions, but requires the modeler to construct a model for each entity. This process, analogous to the knowledge acquisition task in the early days of expert systems, is expensive and time-consuming. Use of simple numerical reasoning as in EINSTein and MANA simplifies the problem, but the modeler still must define the correct personality vector for each fighter.

Closure. While agent-based models are useful tools, they are not the only methods available for predicting a conflict. For example, one might want to incorporate estimates from a Bayesian reasoner or other statistical techniques. Because of the cost of fitting individual units, one might want to approximate the larger context for a conflict with a game-theoretic or Lanchester model, and use agent-based modeling only for a specific engagement.

Dynamism. Models have traditionally been used as a planning tool, in preparation for an engagement. They show how the world might unfold, but once it actually begins to unfold, their detailed results quickly become out of date. One would like to couple model execution to a stream of information from the developing battle and use the model as a real-time monitoring tool, along the lines of model-based control techniques in industrial applications [3].

Singularity. The strength of agent-based models (capturing individual interactions) is also a weakness. A single run of a model captures only one possible evolution of the world. If the number of entities is n and the model is run for t time steps, the number of possible trajectories can be on the order of nt, far too large to be sampled adequately even by many repeated runs, each yielding a single trajectory [17].

A new modeling structure, the polyagent, offers solutions to these challenges.

3. Polyagent Combat Simulation

A polyagent represents a single domain entity with multiple agents: one persistent avatar, which constructs and maintains a model of the entity of interest, and a swarm of transient ghosts, which explore multiple possible futures for that entity. This architecture represents a further step in the direction already taken by agent-based modeling of decomposing the reasoning process. Lanchester equations and game theory aggregated the reasoning about many entities in a single process. Agent-based models give each entity its own process. The polyagent assigns several processes to each entity. This technique has been applied successfully in several military applications. After outlining the architecture in more detail, we consider two examples: self-routing Uninhabited Air Vehicles (UAVs), and urban battle prediction.

3.1. The Architecture

Polyagents coordinate their actions through digital pheromones, scalar variables that agents deposit and sense at their current location in the environment [4, 16, 20, 22, 25]. Such an architecture is called "stigmergic," a biological term that describes how social insects coordinate their actions by leaving and sensing signs in a shared environment [8]. Our stigmergic architecture has three components: polyagents, digital pheromones, and place agents.

Each physical entity is represented by a software polyagent [18]. A polyagent consists of a single persistent avatar and a swarm of transient ghosts that the avatar generates. The avatar maintains a model of the entity (such as a UAV or a warfighter) and manages the dynamics of the ghosts. The ghosts move through the environment, exploring alternative behaviours for their entity. The avatars and ghosts continuously deposit pheromones at their current locations. Polyagents were first demonstrated in factory scheduling [4]. In addition to the military applications discussed in this paper, we are also applying them to problems of intelligence analysis.

Different classes of agents deposit distinct pheromone flavours in their environment. Agents can sense nearby pheromones. Brueckner [4] develops the underlying mathematics of the pheromone field, including critical stability theorems.

The environment takes the form of a distributed network of place agents. These place agents maintain the pheromone field, executing three processes. Aggregation fuses information across multiple agents and through time. Diffusion shares information with nearby agents. Evaporation provides efficient truth maintenance, automatically removing any information that is not reinforced. These processes, together with the feedback when agents both deposit and sense the field, support complex patterns of interaction and coordination among the agents [19]. Each place agent is responsible for a region of the physical space. We tile the physical space with squares or hexagons, each represented by a place agent with four (respectively, six) neighbours, but irregular tiling schemes (such as a Voronoi tessellation defined by the locations of unattended ground sensors) can be employed. Place agents can be situated physically in the environment using unattended ground sensors distributed over an area and connected to nearest neighbours through a wireless network. They may also be located in a distributed network of command and control nodes.

The response of agents to the multiple pheromones in their vicinity is inspired by the personalities of the agents in EINSTein and MANA, described in the previous section. The personality vectors in MANA and EINSTein reflect both rational and emotive aspects of decision-making. The notion of being attracted or repelled by friendly or adversarial forces in various states of health is an important component of what we informally think of as emotion (e.g., fear, compassion, aggression), and the use of the term "personality" in both EINSTein and MANA suggests that the system designers are thinking anthropomorphically, though they do not use "emotion" to describe the effect they are trying to achieve.

The notion of waypoints to which an agent is attracted reflects goal-oriented rationality. An agents personality weights its response to the pheromones it senses through a combining equation. In the simplest form, this combining equation is just the dot product of the personality with the pheromone vector, though more complex forms are sometimes useful. The agent evaluates the combining equation for each movement or action alternative, and selects among the options on the basis of these scores (usually stochastically, with a probability that is weighted by the score).

3.2. Polyagents for Route Planning

[1] Consider an unmanned air vehicle (UAV) that must find its way around a network of surface-to-air missiles in order to reach a target. Fig. 2 shows one possible configuration, in which a gauntlet of threats guards access to the target.

---

[1]This work was supported by the DARPA JFACC program, and reported in [26] and elsewhere.

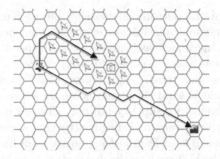

FIGURE 2. Path planning with threats (radar icons) and target (house icon with 'C'.)

A common mechanism in robotics for path planning in this kind of problem is to define a loss function at each point in space on the basis of proximity to threats and targets, integrate it to generate a potential field, and then climb the fields gradient [24]. Such methods require centralized computation, and so do not meet the applicability criterion for a distributed problem. They can also have difficulty solving configurations such as Fig. 2. The field can easily achieve a local maximum outside of the gauntlet, trapping the hill-climbing search prematurely. In one experiment, researchers could only solve this configuration with standard potential methods by first manually defining a waypoint at the entrance to the gauntlet, and then planning the path in two segments, one from the base to the waypoint and the other from the waypoint to the target. Our approach exploits the recognized ability of stochasticity to break out of such local optima (as, for example, in simulated annealing [10]).

This potential-based method is similar to the path-planning mechanisms used in current raster-based GIS systems [6]. In general, these systems develop three successive layers:

1. a "friction" or cost of traversal for each cell, analogous to the loss function used in robotic navigation;
2. the accumulated cost to reach each cell from a specified origin (the minimal path integral of the friction layer from the origin to each cell);
3. the least-cost direction from each cell toward the specified origin, developed by moving perpendicularly to iso-cost contours in the accumulated cost layer.

In this form, the algorithm does not recognize direction-dependent differences in the cost of crossing a cell. This difficulty has been addressed in various ways, including graph-theoretic flow algorithms [28], and iteration [5].

In our approach, an avatar representing a vehicle plans its route by using ghosts to explore alternatives. Both avatars and their ghosts follow the gradient of a function computed over the pheromones in their vicinity. We will shortly describe the stochastic algorithm that ghosts use to follow this gradient. The ghosts on average tend to climb the pheromone gradient, but each explores a slightly different path. A polyagents multiple stochastic ghosts thus reason about alternative possible experiences of the vehicle as it moves through space. The world is not deterministic, and plans (such as pre-planned paths) are rarely followed completely. Particularly in military operations, it is a truism that "no plan survives contact with the enemy." A sudden wind shear may force an aircraft off-course. A robot traveling along the contour of a slippery hill may slide off its planned trajectory. A previously unknown adversary may begin attacking a convoy, requiring it to detour. Such variations can transfer a moving entity from its pre-planned path to a location from which the best path to the destination is no longer the same as the one originally planned. The swarming ghost agents explore many such alternative paths, and the density of the aggregate pheromone field that they generate is a probabilistic balance between the theoretical optimal path and the variation that may be forced on the entity as it travels.

Battlefield intelligence from sensors and reconnaissance activities causes the instantiation of red[2] agents representing known targets and threats. These agents deposit pheromones on the places representing their location in the battlespace. The field they generate is dynamic, since targets and threats can move, new ones can be identified, or old ones can disappear or be destroyed. A blue avatar representing a UAV is associated with one place agent at any given time. It follows the pheromone path created by its ghost agents.

Ghosts initially wander through the network of place agents, attracted to pheromones deposited by targets and repelled by threat pheromones. Once they find a target, they return over the network of place agents to the walker, depositing pheromones that contribute to building the shortest, safest path to the target. The basic pheromone flavors are *RTarget* (deposited by a Red target agent, such as the Red headquarters), *RThreat*(deposited by a Red threat avatar, such as an air defense installation), *GTarget* (deposited by a ghost that has encountered a target and is returning to its blue avatar, forming the path to the target), and *GNest* (deposited by a ghost that has left the blue avatar and is seeking a target).

A ghost agent chooses its next sector stochastically by spinning a roulette wheel with six weighted segments (one for each of its six neighbors). The size of each segment is a function of the strength of the pheromones and is designed to guide the ghost according to the algorithm above. We experimented with several different forms of the combining equation that generates the segment sizes. Manual manipulation yielded the current form (for outbound ghosts):

$$F_n = \frac{\theta \cdot RTarget_n + \gamma \cdot GTartget_n + \beta}{(\rho \cdot GNest_n + \beta) \cdot (Dist_n + \varphi)^{\delta + \alpha(RThreat_n + 1)} + \beta} \qquad (3.1)$$

F_n is the resultant attractive force exerted by neighbor n and *Dist* is the distance to the target if it is known. Table 1 lists the tuneable parameters in the equation and the effect that increasing the parameter has on the ghost's behavior.

---

[2]Following US military custom, we denote the adversary as red, friendly forces as blue, and neutral units (such as civilians) as "green."

Parameter	Effect on Ghost
α	Increases threat avoidance farther from the target
δ	Increases probability of ghosts moving towards a known target in the absence of *RTarget* pheromone
φ	Increases threat avoidance near target
ρ	Increases ghost exploration (by avoiding *GhostNest* pheromone)
θ	Increases attraction to *RTarget* pheromone
β	Avoids division by zero

TABLE 1. Tuneable parameters and their effects on path planning ghosts

Though this table provides general guidance to the practitioner, in practice, the emergent dynamics of the interaction of ghost agents with their environment makes it impossible to predict the behavior of the ghosts. Thus tuning the parameters of this or any pheromone equation becomes a daunting task. We use synthetic evolution to adjust these parameters in real time, as the system is operating [13, 25]. As the avatar emits new ghosts, it breeds them from the fittest ghosts that have already returned. Fitness takes into account three characteristics of those ghosts:

1. Ghosts have a fixed lifetime. Ghosts that complete their search faster have longer to breed, and generate more offspring. Thus we favour ghosts that found shorter paths.
2. Ghosts encounter threats during their search. We favour ghosts that found safer paths.
3. Targets differ in value. We favour ghosts that found more valuable targets.

This system is extremely robust and adaptable [20], and has been deployed successfully on physical robots [26]. It can solve the scenario of Fig.1 (among many others). One simulation study [23] compared a swarm of UAVs guided by these techniques with manned reconnaissance aircraft in detecting and destroying surface-to-air missile installations. The polyagent-based UAVs delivered a 3x improvement in the number of targets detected, a 9x improvement in the system exchange ratio, and an 11x improvement in the percentage of targets destroyed.

Polyagent route planning has several benefits in our application domain over the classical potential field algorithm and its GIS analogues.

- The swarming approach is local. It touches only the cells that the ghost agents actually visit, rather than computing fields across the entire space being modelled.
- Because it is local, the swarming approach naturally supports a distributed network of place agents (such as a network of unattended ground sensors with limited communications range and bandwidth). It does not require synchronized computation of successive layers of information, a feature of the

potential field algorithm that makes it much better suited for centralized computation.

- The swarming approach is dynamic. Ghosts are continually emitted by their avatars as the avatars move, and any changes to the landscape during the course of the mission automatically vary the portion of the path not yet traversed. The potential field method plans a complete path based on a snapshot of the terrain being traversed. If the landscape changes, the user must decide whether to continue to use an old path that may no longer be optimal, or recompute a new path.

- The swarming approach is stochastic. The polyagents ghosts explore a range of alternative trajectories for the robot, reflecting the uncertainty of movement in the physical world, and the path that is computed is a weighted combination of these trajectories. The potential field method is deterministic. It reflects the likely experience of the entity that is to follow the path only in the single loss, cost, or friction value that it assigns to its initial raster, and does not account for possible variation in the experience of the entity as it follows the path.

3.3. Polyagents for Battle Planning

The previous application of polyagent combat simulation focused on developing a plan for *friendly forces* in response to externally-provided intelligence about the adversary. Polyagent simulation can also help us anticipate what the enemy will do. In the planning application, the multiple ghosts explored different ways that the future might evolve[3]. In anticipating the adversary, they also evolve a model of the adversary against past observed behavior, and extrapolate that model for generate predictions. We call this system "behavior evolution and extrapolation", or BEE.

The BEEs pheromone flavors include Alive and Dead pheromone for adversaries, friends, and civilians; weapons fire to indicate recent activity; key sites (such as mosques or schools); mobility (reflecting the presence of roads); cover; and level of estimated threat to friend or foe. The agents personality is a vector of seven values in $[-1, +1]$: ProtectRed (the adversary), ProtectBlue (friendly forces), ProtectGreen (civilians), ProtectKeySites, AvoidCombat, AvoidDetection, and Survive. Negative values reverse the sense suggested by the label. For example, a negative value of Protect- Red indicates a desire to harm Red, and an agent with a high positive value of ProtectRed will be attracted to RED-ALIVE, RED-CASUALTY, and MOBILITY pheromone, and will move at maximum speed.

To predict an entitys behavior, we need to learn its personality vector, but we have access only to its external behavior. Fig. 3 shows our approach. Each active entity in the battlespace has a persistent avatar that continuously generates a stream of ghost agents representing itself. Ghosts live on a timeline indexed by τ that begins in the past and runs into the future. τ is offset with respect to the

---

[3]This work was originally supported by the DARPA RAID program, and reported in [14] and elsewhere.

current time t. The timeline is divided into discrete "pages", each representing a successive value of τ. The avatar inserts the ghosts at the insertion horizon. In one instantiation of this system, the insertion horizon is at $\tau - t = -30$, meaning that ghosts are inserted into a page representing the state of the world 30 minutes ago. At the insertion horizon, each ghosts behavioral parameters (desires and dispositions) are sampled from distributions to explore alternative personalities of the entity it represents.

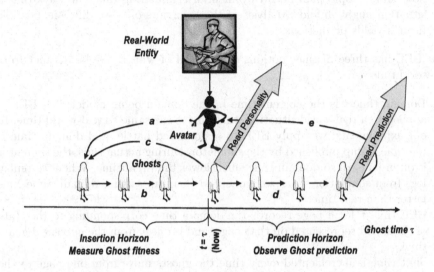

FIGURE 3. Behavioral Evolution and Extrapolation. Each avatar generates (a) a stream of ghosts that sample the personality space of its entity. They evolve (b, c) against the entitys recent observed behavior. The fittest ghosts run into the future (d), and the avatar analyzes their behavior (e) to generate predictions.

Each page between the insertion horizon and $\tau = t$ ("now") records the historical state of the world at the point in the past to which it corresponds. As ghosts move from page to page, they interact with this past state, based on their behavioral parameters. These interactions mean that their fitness depends not just on their own actions, but also on the behaviors of the rest of the population, which is also evolving. Because τ advances faster than real time, eventually $\tau = t$ (actual time). At this point, each ghost is evaluated based on its location compared with the actual location of its corresponding real-world entity.

The fittest ghosts have three functions.

1. The personality of each entitys fittest ghost is reported to the rest of the system as the likely personality of that entity. This information can be used

to detect the emotional state of individual entities [15], or to identify different roles in the adversarial organization.

2. The fittest ghosts breed genetically and their offspring return to the insertion horizon to continue the fitting process.

3. The fittest ghosts for each entity form the basis for a population of ghosts that run past the avatar's present into the future. Each ghost that runs into the future explores a different possible future of the battle, analogous to how some people plan ahead by mentally simulating different ways that a situation might unfold. Analysis of the behaviors of these different possible futures yields predictions.

Thus BEE has three distinct notions of time, all of which may be distinct from real-world time.

1. Domain time t is the current time in the domain being modeled. If BEE is applied to a real-world situation, this time is the same as real-world time. In our experiments, we apply BEE to a simulated battle, and domain time is the time stamp published by the simulator. During actual runs, the simulator is often paused, so domain time runs slower than real time. When we replay logs from simulation runs, we can speed them up so that domain time runs faster than real time.

2. BEE time τ for a page records the domain time corresponding to the state of the world represented on that page, and is offset from the current domain time.

3. Shift time is incremented every time the ghosts move from one page to the next. The relation between shift time and real time depends on the processing resources available.

The distribution of each pheromone flavor over the environment forms a field that represents some aspect of the state of the world at an instant in time. Each page of the timeline is a complete pheromone field for the world at the BEE time τ represented by that page. The behavior of the pheromones on each page depends on whether the page represents the past or the future.

In pages representing the future ($\tau > t$), the usual pheromone mechanisms apply. Ghosts deposit pheromone each time they move to a new page, and pheromones evaporate and propagate from one page to the next.

In pages representing the past ($\tau \leq t$), we have an observed state of the real world. This has two consequences for pheromone management. First, we will have observed some of the entities, and can generate the pheromone fields directly from their observed locations. Second, we can adjust the pheromone intensities based on the changed locations of entities from page to page, so we do not need to evaporate or propagate the pheromones.

Execution of the pheromone infrastructure proceeds on two time scales, running in separate threads.

The first thread updates the book of pages each time the domain time advances past the next page boundary, executing this algorithm at each time step:

```
Replace ''now + 1'' page with page showing locations and
strengths of observed units;

Add empty page at the prediction horizon;

Discard the oldest page (since it has passed the
insertion horizon).
```

The second thread moves the ghosts from one page to the next, as fast as the processor allows, executing the following algorithm at each step:

```
For each ghost reaching the τ = t page

    Evaluate fitness

    Remove or breed

Insert new ghosts from avatars and evolution at insertion horizon


Insert fittest ghosts at τ = t to run into the future

Remove ghosts that have reached the prediction horizon

For each ghost

    Plan next actions based on pheromone field in current page

    Move to next page

    Execute planned actions (including pheromone deposits)

For each future page, evaporate and propagate pheromones
```

Ghost movement based on pheromone gradients is a simple process, so this system can support realistic agent populations without excessive computer load. In our current system, each avatar generates eight ghosts per shift. Since there are about 50 entities in the battlespace (about 20 units each of Red and Blue and about 5 of Green), we must support about 400 ghosts per page, or about 24000 over the entire book.

How fast a processor do we need? Let p be the real-time duration of a page in seconds. If each page represents 60 seconds of domain time, and we are replaying a simulation at 2x domain time, $p = 30$. Let n be the number of pages between the insertion horizon and $τ = t$. In our current system, $n = 30$. Then a shift rate of n/p shifts per second will permit ghosts to run from the insertion horizon to the current time at least once before a new page is generated. Empirically, this level is a lower bound for reasonable performance, and easily achievable on stock WinTel platforms.

The flexibility of the BEEs pheromone infrastructure permits the integration of numerous information sources as input to our characterizations of entity personalities and predictions of their future behavior. Our current system draws on three sources of information, but others can readily be added.

Observations from the real world are encoded into the pheromone field each increment of BEE time, as a new "current page" is generated. Statistical techniques[4] estimate the level of threat to each force (Red or Blue), based on the topology of the battlefield and the known disposition of forces. For example, a broad open area with no cover is threatening, especially if the opposite force occupies its margins. The results of this process are posted to the pheromone pages as "RedThreat" pheromone (representing a threat to red) and "BlueThreat" pheromone (representing a threat to Blue).

While plan recognition is not sufficient for effective prediction, it is a valuable input. We dynamically configure a Bayes net based on heuristics to identify the likely goals that each entity may hold[5]. The destinations of these goals function as "virtual pheromones". Ghosts include their distance to such points in their action decisions, achieving the result of gradient following without the computational expense of maintaining a pheromone field.

The BEE technology performs impressively compared both with human and alternative computational predictors [14].

In one series of wargames, one of the operators controlling a conventional simulation used to evaluate the consequences of players decisions superimposed a coward personality on two units. If they were in a threatening situation, they would ignore the commands issued by the decision-makers and instead flee. Experienced human observers tried to identify which units were the cowards. Fig. 4 shows that our polyagent system was able to identify the cowards as accurately as experienced human officers, but more rapidly.

Fig. 5 shows the superior accuracy of our predictions of the positions of Red units compared with those of human observers. The Wilcoxon test shows that the difference between the H15 scores is significant at the 99.76% level, while that between the H0 scores is significant at more than 99.999%. Fig. 6 shows that our predictions are also more accurate than those produced by a game-theoretic predictor [29].

---

[4]This process, known as SAD (Statistical Anomaly Detection), was developed by our colleagues Rafael Alonso, Hua Li, and John Asmuth at Sarnoff Corporation. Alonso and Li are now at SET Corporation.

[5]This process, known as KIP (Knowledge-based Intention Projection), was developed by our colleagues Paul Nielsen, Jacob Crossman, and Rich Frederiksen at Soar Technology.

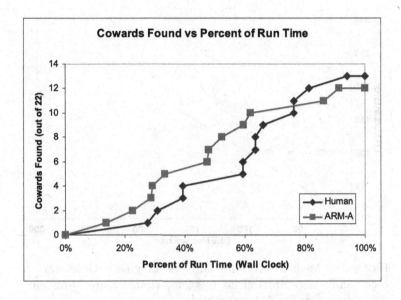

FIGURE 4. BEE vs. Human Emotion Detection.

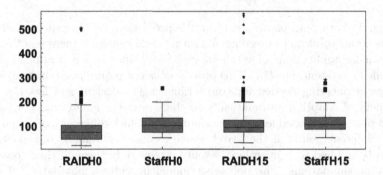

FIGURE 5. Box-and-whisker plots of RAID (BEE) and Staff predictions at 0 and 15 minutes Horizons. Y-axis is CEP radius in meters; lower values indicate greater accuracy.

4. Discussion

Polyagent technology is able to address the challenges of agent-based combat modeling, and offers several promising directions for future research.

4.1. Meeting the Challenges

We identified several challenges faced by current MAS techniques in combat modeling. Polyagents address all of them.

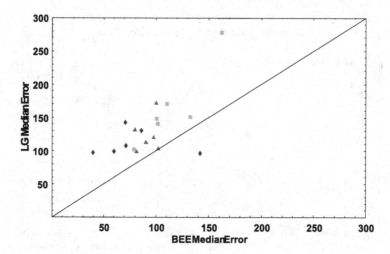

FIGURE 6. Median errors for BEE vs. Linguistic Geometry on each run.Squares are Defend missions, triangles are Move missions, diamonds are Attack missions.

Fitting. In both path planning and battle prediction, we have successfully used synthetic evolution to breed agents rather than configure them manually. Unlike most applications of synthetic evolution, this process is applied on-line, while the system runs [13]. This process does not require the laborious knowledge engineering needed for conventional agent design, and has the added benefit of adapting automatically to changes in the environment. Evolution is a population-based learning mechanism, in which different individuals sample different points in the search space to discover a good configuration. It can be applied to conventional agent systems only through time-consuming off-line simulations. The polyagent model provides a population of agents (the ghosts) all representing the same entity, thus enabling the evolutionary search to proceed while the system runs.

Closure. Our work in battle prediction uses a swarming simulation to integrate inputs from a Bayesian plan recognition system and a statistical threat region detector, as well as to learn agent personalities and predict their future behavior. In principle, this experience suggests that this simulation technique can be extended to serve as a more generic mechanism for integrating multiple modelers, a potential that we are evaluating in further ongoing work.

Dynamism. The simplicity of stigmergic coordination permits a polyagent simulation to execute extremely rapidly. We can run tens of thousands of ghosts on a stock desktop Windows computer fast enough to evolve them and make predictions while keeping up with the real world. In our battle prediction experiments, we receive snapshots of the world every 20 seconds from a separate simulation, which in practical application would be replaced by battlefield sensors.

Singularity. The multiple ghosts in each polyagent concurrently explore multiple possible futures. Each of a polyagents ghosts can interact, through pheromones, with many of the ghosts of other polyagents, in effect sampling multiple alternative interactions in a single run. As a result, a single polyagent run explores multiple possible evolutions of the world, giving a better sense of how representative its outcome is than a conventional MAS with only one agent per entity.

4.2. Further Extensions

The success we have enjoyed with polyagents (in industrial and intelligence applications as well as in military simulation) encourages us to develop and extend the technique. Three of these extensions are the use of a non-spatial environment, sensor planning, and generalization of the architectures application to integrating multiple reasoners.

Stigmergic mechanisms such as those used by a polyagents ghosts require a structured environment in which agents can have a location and with which they can interact locally. In both of the applications discussed in this chapter, the environment is spatial, a regular lattice of place agents that tiles the two-dimensional manifold of the earths surface. Many domains would profit from the ability to develop plans and make predictions over non-spatial structures such as semantic networks and social networks. Unlike lattices, these networks exhibit small-world structure [33], in which distances are not well defined. In spite of this limitation, we have had encouraging results in preliminary experiments in such topologies.

The plans and predictions generated by our systems are currently used by humans. A natural next step is to integrate our reasoning into a closed-loop system. For example, predictions on where the adversary might be could automatically deploy sensors in that area, and feedback from those sensors would then update the predictor.

Perhaps the most broadly applicable extension is generalizing the notion of using a simulation to integrate multiple reasoners. Many reasoners can express their results either through a field over some topology, or by describing the behavior of some process executing over the topology. The first class of results lends itself to representation as a pheromone field, while the second can be translated directly into ghost personalities. The BEEs evolutionary loop can automatically assess the usefulness of such results in modeling observed behavior, integrating them into an overall result and adjusting the relative prominence given to the various inputs as the external situation evolves.

References

[1] I. Balogh and G. Harless, "An Overview of the COMBAT XXI Simulation Model: A Model for the Analysis of Land and Amphibious Warfare," in *Proc. of 71st Military Operations Research Society Symposium*, USMCB Quantico, VA, 2003. http://www.mors.org/publications/abstracts/71morss/wg31_abs.htm.

[2] S. Bonder and L. W. Farrell, *Development of Models for Defense Systems Planning.* SRL 2147 TR70-2, Systems Research Laboratory, University of Michigan, Ann Arbor, MI, 1970.

[3] C. Brosilow and B. Joseph, *Techniques of Model-Based Control.* Upper Saddle River, NJ, Prentice Hall PTR, 2002.

[4] S. Brueckner, *Return from the Ant: Synthetic Ecosystems for Manufacturing Control.* Dr.rer.nat. Thesis at Humboldt University Berlin, Department of Computer Science, 2000. http://dochost.rz.hu-berlin.de/dissertationen/brueckner-sven-2000-06- 21/PDF/Brueckner.pdf.

[5] W. Collischonn and J. V. Pilar, "A direction dependent least-cost-path algorithm for roads and canals," *International Journal of Geographical Information Science*, 14(4), pp. 397-406, 2000.

[6] D. H. Douglas, "Least-cost path in GIS using an accumulated cost surface and slope lines," *Cartographica*, 31:37-51, 1994.

[7] Eternal Egypt. Model of Soldiers of Mesehti, Egyptian Pikemen. 2005. http://www.eternalegypt.org/EternalEgyptWebsiteWeb/HomeServlet?ee_website_action_ key=action.display.element&story_id=5&module_id=31&language_id=1&element_id=6 0577.

[8] P.-P. Grass, "La Reconstruction du nid et les Coordinations Inter-Individuelles chez Bellicositermes Natalensis et Cubitermes sp. La thorie de la Stigmergie: Essai d'interprtation du Comportement des Termites Constructeurs," *Insectes Sociaux*, 6:41-84, 1959.

[9] A. Ilachinski, *Artificial War: Multiagent-based Simulation of Combat.* Singapore, World Scientific, 2004.

[10] S. Kirkpatrick, C. D. Gelatt, and M. P. Vecchi, "Optimization by Simulated Annealing," *Science*, 220:671-80, 1983.

[11] F. W. Lanchester, *Aircraft in Warfare: The Dawn of the Fourth Arm.* London, Constable and Co, Ltd., 1916.

[12] M. K. Lauren and R. T. Stephen, "Map-Aware Non-uniform Automata (MANA)A New Zealand Approach to Scenario Modelling," *Journal of Battlefield Technology*, 5(1 (March)):27ff, 2002. http://www.argospress.com/jbt/Volume5/5-1-4.htm.

[13] H. V. D. Parunak, "Evolving Swarming Agents in Real Time," in *Proc. of Genetic Programming Theory and Practice (GPTP05)*, Ann Arbor, MI, Springer, 2005. http://www.newvectors.net/staff/parunakv/GPTP05.pdf.

[14] H. V. D. Parunak, "Real-Time Agent Characterization and Prediction," in *Proc. of International Joint Conference on Autonomous Agents and Multi-Agent Systems (AAMAS'07)*, Industrial Track, Honolulu, Hawaii, pp. 1421-1428, ACM, 2007. http://www.newvectors.net/staff/parunakv/AAMAS07Fitting.pdf.

[15] H. V. D. Parunak, R. Bisson, S. Brueckner, R. Matthews, and J. Sauter, "Representing Dispositions and Emotions in Simulated Combat," in *Proc. of Workshop on Defence Applications of Multi-Agent Systems (DAMAS05, at AAMAS05)*, Utrecht, Netherlands, pp. 51-65, Springer, 2005. http://www.newvectors.net/staff/parunakv/DAMAS05DETT.pdf.

[16] H. V. D. Parunak and S. Brueckner, "Ant-Like Missionaries and Cannibals: Synthetic Pheromones for Distributed Motion Control," in *Proc. of Fourth International Conference on Autonomous Agents (Agents 2000)*, Barcelona, ES, pp. 467-474, 2000. http://www.newvectors.net/staff/parunakv/MissCann.pdf.

[17] H. V. D. Parunak and S. Brueckner, "Concurrent Modeling of Alternative Worlds with Polyagents," in *Proc. of the Seventh International Workshop on Multi-Agent-Based Simulation (MABS06, at AAMAS06)*, Hakodate, Japan, Springer, 2006. http://www.newvectors.net/staff/parunakv/MABS06Polyagents.pdf.

[18] H. V. D. Parunak and S. Brueckner, "Modeling Uncertain Domains with Polyagents," in *Proc. of International Joint Conference on Autonomous Agents and Multi-Agent Systems (AAMAS'06)*, Hakodate, Japan, ACM, 2006. http://www.newvectors.net/staff/parunakv/AAMAS06Polyagents.pdf.

[19] H. V. D. Parunak, S. Brueckner, M. Fleischer, and J. Odell, "A Design Taxonomy of Multi-Agent Interactions," in *Proc. of Agent-Oriented Software Engineering IV*, Melbourne, AU, pp. 123-137, Springer, 2003. www.newvectors.net/staff/parunakv/cox.pdf.

[20] H. V. D. Parunak, S. Brueckner, and J. Sauter, "Digital Pheromones for Coordination of Unmanned Vehicles," in *Proc. of Workshop on Environments for Multi-Agent Systems (E4MAS 2004)*, New York, NY, pages 246-263, Springer, 2004. http://www.newvectors.net/staff/parunakv/E4MAS04_UAVCoordination.pdf.

[21] H. V. D. Parunak, S. Brueckner, and R. Savit, "Universality in Multi-Agent Systems," in *Proc. of Third International Joint Conference on Autonomous Agents and Multi- Agent Systems (AAMAS 2004)*, New York, NY, pp. 930-937, ACM, 2004. http://www.newvectors.net/staff/parunakv/AAMAS04Universality.pdf.

[22] H. V. D. Parunak, S. A. Brueckner, and J. Sauter, "Digital Pheromone Mechanisms for Coordination of Unmanned Vehicles," in *Proc. of First International Conference on Autonomous Agents and Multi-Agent Systems (AAMAS 2002)*, Bologna, Italy, pp. 449-450, ACM, 2002. www.newvectors.net/staff/parunakv/AAMAS02ADAPTIV.pdf.

[23] H. V. D. Parunak, M. Purcell, and R. O'Connell, "Digital Pheromones for Autonomous Coordination of Swarming UAV's," in *Proc. of First AIAA Unmanned Aerospace Vehicles, Systems, Technologies, and Operations Conference*, Norfolk, VA, AIAA, 2002. www.newvectors.net/staff/parunakv/AIAA02.pdf.

[24] E. Rimon and D. E. Kodischek, "Exact Robot Navigation Using Artificial Potential Functions," *IEEE Transactions on Robotics and Automation*, 8(5 (October)), pp. 501-518, 1992.

[25] J. A. Sauter, R. Matthews, H. V. D. Parunak, and S. Brueckner, "Evolving Adaptive Pheromone Path Planning Mechanisms," in *Proc. of Autonomous Agents and Multi- Agent Systems (AAMAS02)*, Bologna, Italy, pages 434-440, ACM, 2002. www.newvectors.net/staff/parunakv/AAMAS02Evolution.pdf.

150 H.V.D. Parunak

[26] J. A. Sauter, R. Matthews, H. V. D. Parunak, and S. Brueckner, "Performance of Digital Pheromones for Swarming Vehicle Control," in *Proc. of Fourth International Joint Conference on Autonomous Agents and Multi-Agent Systems*, Utrecht, Netherlands, pp. 903-910, ACM, 2005. http://www.newvectors.net/staff/parunakv/AAMAS05SwarmingDemo.pdf.

[27] N. M. Shnerb, Y. Louzoun, E. Bettelheim, and S. Solomon, "The importance of being discrete: Life always wins on the surface," in *Proc. Natl. Acad. Sci. USA*, 97(19 (September 12)), pp. 10322-10324, 2000. http://www.pnas.org/cgi/reprint/97/19/10322.

[28] E. Stefanakis and M. Kavouras, "On the determination of the optimum path in space," in *Proc. of The European Conference on Spatial Information Theory (COSIT 95)*, Semmering, Austria, Springer, 1995.

[29] B. Stilman, *Linguistic Geometry: From Search to Construction*. Boston, Kluwer, 2000.

[30] US Army PEO STRI. OneSAF Objective System (OOS). 2007. http://www.peostri.army.mil/PRODUCTS/ONESAF/.

[31] J. von Neumann, "Zur Theorie der Gesellschaftsspiele'," *Mathematische Annalen*, 100, pp. 295-320, 1928.

[32] J. von Neumann and O. Morgenstern, *Theory of Games and Economic Behavior*. Princeton, Princeton University Press, 1944.

[33] D. J. Watts and S. H. Strogatz, "Collective dynamics of "small-world" networks," *Nature*, 393(6684 (4 June)), pp. 440-442, 1998.

[34] Wikipedia. Kriegspiel (wargame). 2007.

[35] Wikipedia. Lotka-Volterra equation. 2007. http://en.wikipedia.org/wiki/Lotka-Volterra_equation.

[36] W. G. Wilson, "Resolving Discrepancies between Deterministic Population Models and Individual-Based Simulations," *American Naturalist*, 151(2), pp. 116-134, 1998.

H. Van Dyke Parunak
NewVectors
3520 Green Court, Suite 250
Ann Arbor, MI, 48105-1579
USA
e-mail: van.parunak@newvectors.net

Whitestein Series in Software Agent Technologies, 151–166
© 2007 Birkhäuser Verlag Basel/Switzerland

Using Multi-Agent Teams to Improve the Training of Incident Commanders

Nathan Schurr and Milind Tambe

Abstract. The DEFACTO system is a multi-agent based tool for training incident commanders for large scale disasters. While this system is currently used for the command of a disaster response scenario, the lessons learned and the methods used to approach this challenging domain apply directly to military applications such as the command and control of troops. In this paper, we highlight some of the lessons that we have learned from our interaction with the Los Angeles Fire Department (LAFD) and how they have affected the way that we continued the design of our training system. These lessons were gleaned from LAFD feedback and initial training exercises and they include: system design, visualization, improving trainee situational awareness, adjusting training level of difficulty and situation scale. We have taken these lessons and used them to improve the DEFACTO system's training capabilities. We have conducted initial training exercises to illustrate the utility of the system in terms of providing useful feedback to the trainee.

1. Introduction

Recent events around the US have served to reaffirm the need for emergency response agencies to be better prepared for large scale disasters. Both natural and man-made (terrorism) disasters are growing in scale, however the response to these incidents continues to be managed by a single person, namely the incident commander. The incident commander must monitor and direct the entire event while maintaining complete responsibility. Because of this, incident commanders must start to be trained to handle these large scale events and assist in the coordination of the responding team.

This research was supported by the United States Department of Homeland Security through the Center for Risk and Economic Analysis of Terrorism Events (CREATE) under grant number N00014-05-0630. However, any opinions, findings, and conclusions or recommendations in this document are those of the authors and do not necessarily reflect views of the United States Department of Homeland Security.

In order to fulfill this need and leverage the advantages of multi-agents, we have continued to develop the DEFACTO system (Demonstrating Effective Flexible Agent Coordination of Teams via Omnipresence). DEFACTO is a multi-agent based tool for training incident commanders for large scale disasters (man-made or natural). While this system is currently used for the command of a disaster response scenario, the lessons learned and the methods used to approach this challenging domain apply directly to military applications such as the command and control of troops. Similarly, military troops often have to coordinate among these same kinds of dynamics that arise from tackling man-made or natural disasters.

Our system combines a high fidelity simulator, a redesigned human interface, and a multi-agent team driving all of the behaviors. Training incident commanders provides a dynamic scenario in which decisions must be made correctly and quickly because human safety is at risk. When using DEFACTO, incident commanders have the opportunity to see the disaster in simulation and the coordination and resource constraints unfold so that they can be better prepared when commanding over an actual disaster. Applying DEFACTO to disaster response aims to benefit the training of incident commanders in the fire department.

With DEFACTO, our objective is to both enable the human to have a clear idea of the team's state and improve agent-human team performance. We want DEFACTO agent-human teams to better prepare firefighters for current human-only teams. We believe that by leveraging multi-agents, DEFACTO will result in better disaster response methods and better incident commanders.

Previously, we have discussed building our initial prototype system, DE-FACTO [8]. Recently, the Los Angeles Fire Department (LAFD) have begun to evaluate the DEFACTO system. In this paper, we highlight some of the lessons that we have learned from our interaction with the LAFD and how they have affected the way that we continued to design of our training system. These lessons were gleaned from LAFD feedback and initial training exercises.

The lessons learned from the feedback from the LAFD include: system design, visualization, improving trainee situational awareness, adjusting training level of difficulty and situation scale. We have taken these lessons and used them to improve the DEFACTO system's training capabilities.

We have also performed initial training exercise experiments to illustrate the utility of the system in terms of providing useful feedback to the trainee. We ended up finding that allowing more fire engines to be at the disposal of the incident commander sometimes not only didn't improve, but rather worsened team performance. There were even some instances in which the agent team would have performed better had the team never listened to human advice at all. We also provide analysis of such behaviors, thereby illustrating the utility of DEFACTO resulting from the feedback given to trainees.

(a) Current Incident Commander Training Exercise (b) Fire Captain Roemer using the DE-FACTO training system

FIGURE 1. Old vs. New training methods

2. Motivation

In this section, we will first start with an explanation of the current methods for training that the LAFD currently use. Then we explain some of the advantages that our multi-agent approach has over these methods.

The incident commander's main duties during a fire shoulder all responsibility for the safety of the firefighters. In order to do this, the incident commander must have constant contact with the firefighters and have a complete picture of the entire situation. The incident commander must make certain that dangerous choices are avoided and the firefighters are informed and directed as needed.

We were allowed to observe a Command Post Exercise that simulated the place where the incident commander is stationed during a fire (see Fig. 1(a)). The Incident commander has an assistant by his side who keeps track on a large sheet of paper where all of the resources (personnel and equipment) are located. A sketch of the fire is also made on this sheet, and the fire and fire engines' location is also managed.

The Command Post is currently simulated by projecting a single static image of a fire in an apartment. In the back of the room, several firefighters are taken off duty in order to play the role of firefighters on the scene. They each communicate on separate channels over walkie talkies in order to coordinate by sharing information and accepting orders. The fire spreading is simulated solely by having one of the off-duty firefighters in the back speaking over the walkie talkie and describing fire spreading.

The LAFD's current approach, however, has several limitations. First, it requires a number of officers to be taken off duty, which decreases the number of resources available to the city for a disaster during training. Second, the disaster conditions created are not accurate in the way that they appear or progress. Since the image that the incident commander is seeing is static, there is no information about state or conditions of the fire that can be ascertained from watching it, which is contrary to the actual scene of a disaster response. Furthermore, the fire's behavior is determined by the reports of the acting fire fighters over the walkie talkie, which at times might not be a plausible progression of fire in reality. Third, this method of training restricts it to a smaller scale of fire because of the limited personnel and rigid fire representation.

Our system aims to enhance the training of the incident commanders (see Fig. 1(b)). Our approach allows for training to not be so personnel heavy, because fire fighter actors will be replaced by agents. By doing this we can start to train incident commanders with a larger team. Through our simulation, we can also start to simulate larger events in order to push the greater number of available resources to their limit. Also, by simulating the fire progression, we can place the incident commander in a more realistic situation and force them to react to realistic challenges that arise.

3. System Architecture

In this section, we will describe the technologies used in three major components of DEFACTO: the Omni-Viewer, proxy-based team coordination, and proxy-based adjustable autonomy. The Omni-Viewer is an advanced human interface for interacting with an agent-assisted response effort. The Omni-Viewer has been introduced before [8], however it has since been redesigned by incorporating lessons learned by interactions with the LAFD. The Omni-Viewer now provides both global and local views of an unfolding situation, allowing a human decision-maker to obtain precisely the information required for a particular decision. A team of completely distributed proxies, where each proxy encapsulates advanced coordination reasoning based on the theory of teamwork, controls and coordinates agents in a simulated environment. The use of the proxy-based team brings realistic coordination complexity to the training system and allows a more realistic assessment of the interactions between humans and agent-assisted response. These same proxies also enable us to implement the adjustable autonomy necessary to balance the decisions of the agents and human. This architecture has been described in a more extended fashion in [8]; we present a brief report here.

DEFACTO operates in a disaster response simulation environment. The simulation environment itself is provided by the RoboCup Rescue Simulator [3]. To interface with DEFACTO, each fire engine is controlled by a proxy in order to handle the coordination and execution of adjustable autonomy strategies. Consequently, the proxies can try to allocate fire engines to fires in a distributed manner, but can also transfer control to the more expert user (incident commander). The user can then use the Omni-Viewer to allocate engines to the fires that he has control over. In our scenario, several buildings are initially on fire, and these fires spread to adjacent buildings if they are not quickly contained. The goal is to have a human interact with the team of fire engines in order to save the greatest number of buildings. Our overall system architecture applied to disaster response can be seen in Fig. 2.

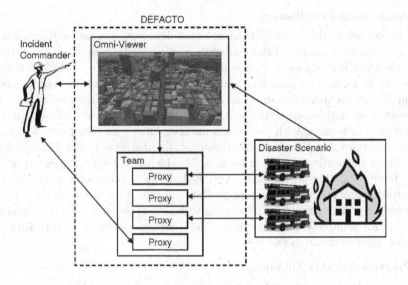

FIGURE 2. System Architecture

3.1. Omni-Viewer

Our goal of allowing fluid human interaction with agents requires a visualization system that provides the human with a global view of agent activity as well as shows the local view of a particular agent when needed. Hence, we have developed an omnipresent viewer, or Omni-Viewer, which will allow the human user diverse interaction with remote agent teams. While a global view is obtainable from a two-dimensional map, a local perspective is best obtained from a 3D viewer, since the 3D view incorporates the perspective and occlusion effects generated by a particular viewpoint.

To address our discrepant goals, the Omni-Viewer allows for both a conventional map-like top down 2D view and a detailed 3D viewer. The viewer shows the global overview as events are progressing and provides a list of tasks that the agents have transferred to the human, but also provides the freedom to move to desired locations and views. In particular, the user can drop to the virtual ground level, thereby obtaining the perspective (local view) of a particular agent. At this level, the user can fly freely around the scene, observing the local logistics involved as various entities are performing their duties. This can be helpful in evaluating the physical ground circumstances and altering the team's behavior accordingly. It also allows the user to feel immersed in the scene where various factors (psychological, etc.) may come into effect.

3.2. Proxy: Team Coordination

A key hypothesis in this work is that intelligent distributed agents will be a key element of a disaster response. Taking advantage of emerging robust, high bandwidth communication infrastructure, we believe that a critical role of these intelligent agents will be to manage coordination between all members of the response team. Specifically, we are using coordination algorithms inspired by theories of teamwork to manage the distributed response [6]. The general coordination algorithms are encapsulated in *proxies*, with each team member having its own proxy which represents it in the team. The current version of the proxies is called *Machinetta* [7] and extends the earlier Teamcore proxies [5]. Machinetta is implemented in Java and is freely available on the web. Notice that the concept of a reusable proxy differs from many other "multi-agent toolkits" in that it provides the coordination *algorithms*, e.g., algorithms for allocating tasks, as opposed to the *infrastructure*, e.g., APIs for reliable communication. These proxies and their architecture have been discussed in detail in [8].

3.3. Proxy: Adjustable Autonomy

One key aspect of the proxy-based coordination is "adjustable autonomy." Adjustable autonomy refers to an agent's ability to dynamically change its own autonomy, possibly to transfer control over a decision to a human. Previous work on adjustable autonomy could be categorized as either involving a single person interacting with a single agent (the agent itself may interact with others) or a single person directly interacting with a team. In the single-agent single-human category, the concept of flexible transfer-of-control strategy has shown promise [6]. A transfer-of-control strategy is a preplanned sequence of actions to transfer control over a decision among multiple entities. For example, an AH_1H_2 strategy implies that an agent (A) attempts a decision and if the agent fails in the decision then the control over the decision is passed to a human H_1, and then if H_1 cannot reach a decision, then the control is passed to H_2. Since previous work focused on single-agent single-human interaction, strategies were individual agent strategies where only a single agent acted at a time.

An optimal transfer-of-control strategy optimally balances the risks of not getting a high quality decision against the risk of costs incurred due to a delay in getting that decision. Flexibility in such strategies implies that an agent dynamically chooses the one that is optimal, based on the situation, among multiple such strategies (H_1A, AH_1, AH_1A, etc.) rather than always rigidly choosing one strategy. The notion of flexible strategies, however, has not been applied in the context of humans interacting with agent-teams. Thus, a key question is whether such flexible transfer of control strategies are relevant in agent-teams, particularly in a large-scale application such as ours.

DEFACTO has introduced the notion of team-level adjustable autonomy strategies. For example, rather than transferring control from a human to a single agent, a team-level strategy could transfer control from a human to any one of the members of the agent-team. Consequently, a distinct transfer of control may occur for each team task that can transfer between the human and an agent teammate. Concretely, each proxy is provided with all strategy options; the key is to select the right strategy given the situation. An example of a team level strategy would combine A_T Strategy and H Strategy in order to make $A_T H$ Strategy. The default team strategy, A_T, keeps control over a decision with the agent team for the entire duration of the decision. The H strategy always immediately transfers control to the human. $A_T H$ strategy is the conjunction of team level A_T strategy with H strategy. This strategy aims to significantly reduce the burden on the user by allowing the decision to first pass through all agents before finally going to the user, if the agent team fails to reach a decision.

4. Lessons Learned from Initial Deployment Feedback

Through our communication with strategic training division of the LAFD (see Fig. 1(b)), we have learned a lot of lessons that have influenced the continuing development of our system.

4.1. Adjustable Autonomy in Practice

Our most important lesson learned from talking with the LAFD and seeing their exercises is that adjustable autonomy correctly maps over to what happens in the actual disaster response. The adjusting of autonomy is easily seen as the event scales up and down in size and intensity. For a smaller scale response to, for example, a residential single story house fire, the incident commander will usually make all allocation decisions and thus practice the A strategy. For a larger scale event, a lot of the burden of most allocations are left to the team and other entities in the hierarchy, while the Incident Commander is left to concentrate on the bigger picture. In this case, the Incident commander is notified if a specifically problematic situation occurs, for example not enough resources to attack a particular fire. This strategy is essentially what we refer to as $A_T H$ in our experiments, in which, the team first tries to assign someone to the fire with the resources they have, and if not able to then pass it off to the Incident Commander for help. If the situation were to die down and the size of the team were to decrease, more autonomy would be shifted to the Incident Commander due to an increased ability to make allocations for the team.

It is very helpful to know that these strategies not only are capable of making our agent teams perform well and interface with the incident commander, but that they also reflect similar strategies that current firefighting teams are using.

4.2. Questioning the Incident Commander

Another lesson that relates to our agent design is that we learned how a team on the ground may possibly not agree with the command (allocation to a fire) given by the incident commander. This will usually be due to the fact that the incident commander has a broad global view of the disaster, whereas the agents each have a more detailed local view. This mismatch in information can, at times, lead to

(a) Local Perspective   (b) Global Perspective

FIGURE 3. Local vs. Global Perspectives in the Omni-Viewer

detrimental team allocations. In an actual disaster response, this is handled by the allocated team both questioning the order and providing the incident commander with the missing information.

This has led us to consider a team of agents that can disagree with human inputs. This issue has not been addressed in our implementation as of yet, but it is relevant given the results that will be presented later in the training exercise experiments. There are experimental settings in which the team performance would have been improved, had they rejected the incident commander's input.

4.3. Perspective

Just as in multi-agent systems, the incident commander must overcome the challenge of managing a team that each possess only a partial local view. This is highlighted in fighting a fire by incident commanders keeping in mind that when a firefighter arrives at a building that is on fire, there are five views to that fire (4 sides of the building and the rooftop). Only by taking into account what is happening on all five sides of the fire, can the fire company make an effective decision on how many people to send where. Because of this, a local view (see Fig. 3(a)) can augment the global view (see Fig. 3(b)) and becomes helpful in determining the local perspectives of team members. For example, by taking the perspective of a fire company in the back of the building, the incident commander can be aware that they might not see the smoke from the second floor, which is only visible from the front of the building. The incident commander can then make a decision to communicate that to the fire company or make an allocation accordingly.

The 3D perspective of the Omni-Viewer was initially thought to be an example of a futuristic vision of the actual view given to the incident commander. But after allowing the fire fighters to look at the display, they remarked, that they have such views available to them already, especially in large scale fires (the very fires we are trying to simulate). At the scene of these fires often a news helicopter is at the scene and the incident commander can patch into the feed and display it at his command post. Consequently our training simulation can already start

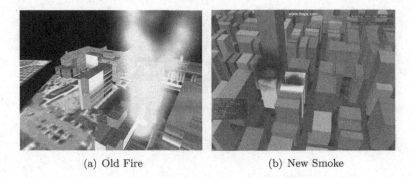

(a) Old Fire (b) New Smoke

FIGURE 4. Improvement in fire visualization

to prepare the incident commander to incorporate a diverse array of information sources.

4.4. Fire Behavior

We also learned how important smoke and fire behavior is to the firefighters in order to affect their decisions. Upon our first showing of initial prototypes to the incident commanders, they looked at our simulation, with flames swirling up out of the roof (see Fig. 4(a)). We artificially increased fire intensity in order to show off the fire behavior and this hampered their ability to evaluate the situation and allocations. They all agreed that every firefighter should be pulled out because that building is lost and might fall at any minute! In our efforts to put a challenging fire in front of them to fight, we had caused them to walk away from the training. Once we start to add training abilities, such as to watch the fire spread in 3D, we have to also start to be more aware of how to accurately show a fire that the incident commander would face. We have consequently altered the smoke and fire behavior (see Fig. 4(b)). The smoke appears less "dramatic" to a lay person than a towering inferno, but it provides a more effective training environment.

4.5. Gradual Training

Initially, we were primarily concerned with changes to the system that allowed for a more accurate simulation of what the incident commander would actually see. Alternatively, we have also added features, not because of their accuracy, but also to aid in training by isolating certain tasks. Very often in reality and in our simulations, dense urban areas obscure the ability to see where all of the resources (i.e., fire engines) are and prevent a quick view of the situation (see Fig. 5(a)). To this aim, we have added a new mode using the 3D, but having the buildings each have no height, which we refer to as Flat World (see Fig. 5(b)). By using this flat view, the trainee is allowed to concentrate on the allocation of resources, without the extra task of developing an accurate world view with obscuring high rise buildings.

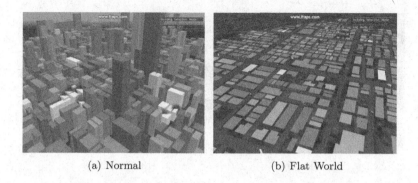

(a) Normal   (b) Flat World

FIGURE 5. Improvement in locating resources (fire engines and ambulances)

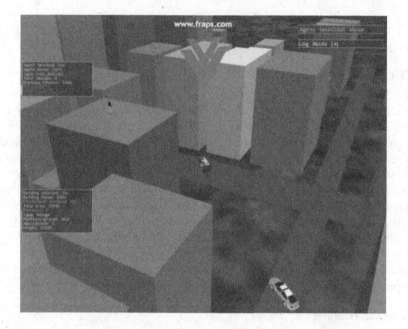

FIGURE 6. Selecting for closer look at a Fire Engine.

4.6. User Intent

A very important lesson that we learned from the LAFD, was that the incident commander cannot be given all information for the team and thus the human does not know all about the status of the team members and vice versa. Consequently, this lack of complete awareness of the agent team's intentions can lead to some harmful allocations by the human (incident commander). In order for information to be selectively available to the incident commander, we have allowed the incident commander to query for the status of a particular agent. Fig. 6 shows an arrow

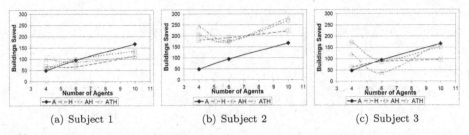

(a) Subject 1   (b) Subject 2   (c) Subject 3

FIGURE 7. Performance.

above the Fire Engine at the center of the screen that has been selected. On the left, the statistics are displayed. The incident commander is able to select a particular fire engine and find out the equipment status, personnel status, and the current tasks that are being performed by the fire fighters aboard that engine. This detailed information can be accessed if desired by the incident commander, but is not thrown to the screen by all agents, in order to not overwhelm the incident commander.

4.7. Scale

In addition, we have also learned of new challenges that we are currently attempting to tackle by enhancing the system. One of the biggest challenges in order to start simulating a large urban fire is the sheer scale of the resources that must be managed. According to the fire captains, in order to respond to a single high rise building with a few floors on fire, roughly 200 resources (fire engines, paramedics etc.) would need to be managed at the scene. Coordinating such a large number of agents on a team is a challenge. Also, as the incident scales to hundreds of resources, the incident commander ends up giving more autonomy to the team or else face being overwhelmed. We believe that adjustable autonomy will start to play a bigger and more essential roll in allowing for the incident commander to monitor the larger situations.

5. Lessons Learned from Training Exercises

In this section, we will present results and analysis from a set of training exercises. Our initial experimental results have been published earlier [8], however the analysis presented here is new.

5.1. Training Exercises

In order to study the potential of DEFACTO, we performed some training exercises with volunteers. These initial experiments showed us that humans can both help and hurt the team performance. The key point is that DEFACTO allows such experiments with training exercises and more importantly allows for analysis and feedback regarding the exercises. Thus trainees can gain useful insight as to why their decisions led to problematic/beneficial situations.

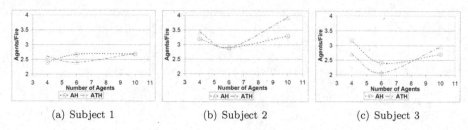

(a) Subject 1   (b) Subject 2   (c) Subject 3

FIGURE 8. Amount of agents assigned per fire.

The results of our training exercise experiments are shown in Fig. 7, which shows the results of subjects 1, 2, and 3. Each subject was confronted with the task of aiding fire engines in saving a city hit by a disaster. For each subject, we tested three strategies, specifically, H, AH (individual agent, then human) and $A_T H$ (agent team, then human); their performance was compared with the completely autonomous A_T strategy. AH is an individual agent strategy, tested for comparison with $A_T H$, where agents act individually, and pass those tasks to a human user that they cannot immediately perform. Each experiment was conducted with the same initial locations of fires and level of building damage. For each strategy that we tested, we varied the number of fire engines between 4, 6 and 10. Each chart in Fig. 7 shows the varying number of fire engines on the x-axis, and the team performance in terms of numbers of buildings saved on the y-axis. For instance, strategy A_T saves 50 buildings with 4 agents. Each data point on the graph is an average of three runs. Each run itself took 15 minutes, and each user was required to participate in 27 experiments, which together with 2 hours of getting oriented with the system, equates to about 9 hours of experiments per volunteer.

Fig. 7 enables us to conclude the following:

- *Human involvement with agent teams does not necessarily lead to improvement in team performance.* Contrary to expectations and prior results, human involvement does not uniformly improve team performance, as seen by human-involving strategies performing worse than the A_T strategy in some cases. For instance, for subject 3 AH strategy provides higher team performance than A_T for 4 agents, yet at 10 agents human influence is clearly not beneficial. Deeper assessment of what lead to this is found in Section 5.2.

- *Providing more agents at a human's command does not necessarily improve the agent team performance.* As seen for subject 2 and subject 3, increasing agents from 4 to 6 given AH and $A_T H$ strategies is seen to degrade performance. In contrast, for the A_T strategy, the performance of the fully autonomous agent team continues to improve with additions of agents, thus indicating that the reduction in AH and $A_T H$ performance is due to human involvement. As the number of agents increase to 10, the agent team does recover.

- *Complex team-level strategies are helpful in practice:* $A_T H$ leads to improvement over H with 4 agents for all subjects, although surprising domination of AH over $A_T H$ in some cases indicates that AH is still a useful strategy to have available in a team setting and should not be completely replaced by $A_T H$.

Note that the phenomena described range over multiple users, multiple runs, and multiple strategies. Unfortunately, the strategies including the humans and agents (AH and $A_T H$) for 6 agents show a noticeable decrease in performance for subjects 2 and 3 (see Fig. 7). It would be useful to understand which factors contributed to this phenomenon from a trainee's perspective.

5.2. Analysis

We decided to perform a more in depth analysis of what exactly was causing the degrading performance when 6 agents were at the disposal of the incident commander. Fig. 8 shows the number of agents on the x-axis and the average amount of fire engines allocated to each fire on the y-axis. AH and $A_T H$ for 6 agents result in significantly less average fire engines per task (fire) and therefore lower average. Another interesting thing that we found was that this lower average was not due to the fact that the incident commander was overwhelmed and making less decisions (allocations). Fig. 9(a), 9(b), and 9(c) all show how the number of buildings attacked do not go down in the case of 6 agents, where poor performance is seen.

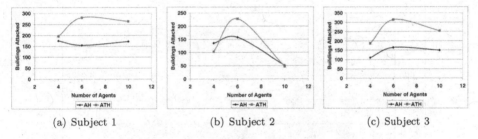

(a) Subject 1   (b) Subject 2   (c) Subject 3

FIGURE 9. Number of buildings attacked.

Fig. 10 and 11 show the number of agents assigned to a building on the x-axis and the probability that the given building would be saved on the y-axis. The correlation between these values demonstrate the correlation between the number of agents assigned and the quality of the decision.

We can conclude from this analysis that the degradation in performance occurred at 6 agents because fire engine teams were split up, leading to fewer fire-engines being allocated per building on average. Indeed, leaving fewer than 3 fire engines per fire leads to a significant reduction in fire extinguishing capability. We can provide such feedback of overall performance, showing the performance reduction at six fire engines, and our analysis to a trainee. The key point here is that DEFACTO is capable of allowing for such exercises, and their analysis, and providing feedback to potential trainees, so they improve their decision making,

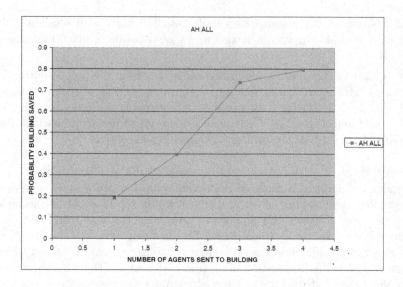

FIGURE 10. AH for all subjects.

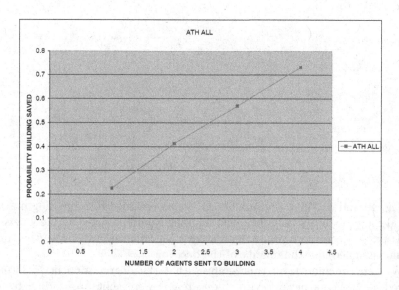

FIGURE 11. ATH for all subjects.

Thus, in this current set of exercises, trainees can understand that with six fire engines, they had managed to split up existing resources inappropriately.

6. Related Work and Summary

In terms of related work, it is important to mention products like JCATS [9] and EPICS [4]. JCATS represents a self-contained, high-resolution joint simulation in use for entity-level training in open, urban and subterranean environments. Developed by Lawrence Livermore National Laboratory, JCATS gives users the capability to detail the replication of small group and individual activities during a simulated operation. At this point however, JCATS cannot simulate agents. Finally, EPICS is a computer-based, scenario-driven, high-resolution simulation. It is used by emergency response agencies to train for emergency situations that require multi-echelon and/or inter-agency communication and coordination. Developed by the U.S. Army Training and Doctrine Command Analysis Center, EPICS is also used for exercising communications and command and control procedures at multiple levels. Similar to JCATS however, EPICS does not currently allow agents to participate in the simulation. More recently multi-agents have been successfully applied to training navy tactics [10] and teams of Uninhabited Air Vehicles [1, 2]. Our work is similar to these in spirit, however our focus and lessons learned are based on the train of incident commanders in disaster rescue environments.

In summary, in order to train incident commanders for large scale disasters, we have been working on the DEFACTO training system. This multi-agent system tool has begun to be used by fire captains from the Los Angeles Fire Department. We have learned some valuable lessons from their feedback and the analysis of some initial training exercise experiments. These lessons were gleaned from LAFD feedback and initial training exercises. The lessons learned from the feedback from the LAFD include: system design, visualization, improving trainee situational awareness, adjusting training level of difficulty and situation scale. We have taken these lessons and used them to improve the DEFACTO system's training abilities. We have conducted initial training exercises to illustrate the utility of the system in terms of providing useful feedback to the trainee. Through DEFACTO, we hope to improve training tools for and consequently improve the preparedness of incident commanders.

7. Acknowledgments

Thanks to CREATE center for their support. Thanks to Pratik Patil and Fred Pighin for their help with the Omni-Viewer. Also, thanks to Fire Captains of the LAFD: Ronald Roemer, David Perez, and Roland Sprewell for their time and invaluable input to this project.

References

[1] J. W. Baxter and G. S. Horn, "Controlling teams of uninhabited air vehicles," in *Proceedings of the fourth international joint conference on Autonomous agents and multiagent systems (AAMAS)*, 2005.

[2] S. Karim and C. Heinze, "Experiences with the design and implementation of an agent-based autonomous uav controller," in *Proceedings of the fourth international joint conference on Autonomous agents and multiagent systems (AAMAS)*, 2005.

[3] H. Kitano, S. Tadokoro, I. Noda, H. Matsubara, T. Takahashi, A. Shinjoh, and S. Shimada, "Robocup rescue: Search and rescue in large-scale disasters as a domain for autonomous agents research," in *IEEE SMC*, volume VI, pages 739–743, Tokyo, October 1999.

[4] L. L. N. Laboratory, "Jcats - joint conflict and tactical simulation," in *http://www.jfcom.mil/about/fact_jcats.htm*, 2005.

[5] D. V. Pynadath and M. Tambe, "Automated teamwork among heterogeneous software agents and humans," *Journal of Autonomous Agents and Multi-Agent Systems (JAAMAS)*, 7:71–100, 2003.

[6] P. Scerri, D. Pynadath, and M. Tambe, "Towards adjustable autonomy for the real world," *Journal of Artificial Intelligence Research*, 17:171–228, 2002.

[7] P. Scerri, D. V. Pynadath, L. Johnson, P. Rosenbloom, N. Schurr, M. Si, and M. Tambe, "A prototype infrastructure for distributed robot-agent-person teams," In *AAMAS*, 2003.

[8] N. Schurr, J. Marecki, P. Scerri, J. P. Lewis, and M. Tambe, "The defacto system: Training tool for incident commanders," In *The Seventeenth Innovative Applications of Artificial Intelligence Conference (IAAI)*, 2005.

[9] A. S. Technology, "Epics - emergency preparedness incident commander simulation," In *http://epics.astcorp.com*, 2005.

[10] W. A. van Doesburg, A. Heuvelink, and E. L. van den Broek, "Tacop: A cognitive agent for a naval training simulation environment," in *Proceedings of the fourth international joint conference on Autonomous agents and multiagent systems (AAMAS)*, 2005.

Nathan Schurr and Milind Tambe
University of Southern California
Los Angeles, CA 90089
USA
e-mail: schurr@usc.edu
       tambe@usc.edu